STREAM LINE

HOW TO CREATE
HEALTHY CHURCH SYSTEMS

MICHAEL
LUKASZEWSKI

1

CAUFIELD AND FINCH
Streamline: How to Create Healthy Church Systems
Michael Lukaszewski

Copyright © 2016 by Michael Lukaszewski
All Rights Reserved

Copyeditor: Keidi Keating
Cover Design: Canvas Agency
Interior Design: Aaron Skinner
Interior Layout: Kristin Gelinas

Published in the United States by Caufield and Finch
ISBN 978-09965162-0-4

First Edition

Also by Michael Lukaszewski

No Matter What: Ten Things I Want My Children to Know

From the Top Down: The Nuts and Bolts of Launching and
Leading a Church

FOR PASTORS EVERYWHERE

WHO LEAD WHEN THEY ARE TIRED,

PREACH BECAUSE THEY MUST,

HOPE WHEN THINGS ARE HOPELESS,

AND BELIEVE THE UNBELIEVABLE.

TABLE OF CONTENTS

INTRODUCTION

WHAT'S AT STAKE?

To be in hell is to drift; to be in heaven is to steer.

- George Bernard Shaw -

You are confident of your calling. You are leading a church with an important mission. You have a carefully worded vision statement, a set of core values, and leaders who say they want to make it happen.

But does it feel like you're not making any real progress? Does it feel like you're stuck solving the same problems over and over again? Does it seem that you're always talking about potential, or tomorrow, or after the next hire?

After twenty years in ministry, I've learned passion isn't enough.

You can have a clear mission, but without organization you won't get everyone moving in the right direction. You can preach the vision, but if you don't have a clear path ready for people, your vision talk will be just talk.

I bet you don't have a mission problem, or a facility problem, or even a volunteer problem. I know it's trendy to talk multi-site, and popular to run a 40 day campaign. New service times, new programs, and new websites are like candy that captures attention in the checkout aisle.

But it's likely these aren't the issues holding you back. You can start new services and hire a branding company to create a new website, and in three years from now you'll likely be in the same place.

That's because you're knee deep in a system problem.

I've spoken to pastors struggling to get off the ground and pastors leading churches on the fastest growing lists. I've spoken to hundreds of church leaders about what's working and what's not working in their churches. And I've seen firsthand what can happen when systems, strategies, and tools intersect with a Spirit-led congregation.

Even if I've never been to your church, here's what I know:

1. **Good systems don't naturally develop in a church.** We know from High School physics that things go from a state of order to disorder. In other words, things get worse over time...they don't get better. The same is true of your church. You may have been organized in the past, but that doesn't mean you're organized now. Things may have worked well yesterday, but they won't stay that way without the implementation of fresh strategies.

2. **Good systems solve problems.** Many of the problems you face in your church are system problems. If you have a virus in the computer, it affects every program. But when you pay attention to the system, some of the problems will solve themselves.

3. **Systems often determine success.** Andy Stanley says your system is perfectly designed to get the results you're getting. Working harder or communicating better won't solve all of your problems. In fact, those things *rarely* solve

problems. You have to fix the broken system if you want different results.

4. **Good systems lead to better decisions.** Getting organized will give you the time and space you need to do better. When you get organized, you'll find that you make better decisions.

5. **Organization will save you money.** This is where all the church planters start paying attention! If you install some good systems in your church, you'll save real money.

Passion isn't enough and vision isn't enough. You have to organize and align everything if you want to see fruit. You have to bring some systems and structure to the passion and vision. Then, you will have a powerful combination. Then, you will streamline the church.

HOW A YOUTH PASTOR BECOMES THE SYSTEMS GUY

Like Haley Joel Osmond, I'm typecast. Somewhere along the way, I was labeled a church systems guy. From someone who started his ministry career as a youth pastor and then became a church planter, this is pretty funny. It's not like youth pastors are known for their wildly successful organizational tactics.

In 2005, after a dozen years of working with students, my family and I moved from Arkansas to Atlanta to start a new church. With a team of 25 committed people, we launched in a movie theater. The church grew quickly in that first year—from a small group of people to over eight hundred on our one year anniversary.

Church planting years are like dog years. So this was like a cute little puppy growing into a 100 pound guard dog overnight.

A little after that one year mark, I had a mini-crisis because I realized we didn't have any systems in place to deal with the rapid growth. We succeeded in getting people to church, but we hadn't answered the question, "What's next?" How were we going to disciple these people? How would we move them to groups? How would we follow up with guests and givers? I knew how to attract a crowd, but I knew little about leading a church.

I'd get mad at problems and throw a little of my attention at them. But they would come back time and time again. We patched it when it was broken, but it would only break again. We treated the symptom but never addressed the broken system. We could get people to come to church, but as a church, we couldn't get traction.

We didn't have healthy systems to sustain growth. As a visionary leader who loved preaching and leading, the idea of creating systems and flow charts sounded like it was as exciting as going to the dentist. Both are necessary.

If you're attracting people, but not keeping people, you have a systems problem. If you're launching programs, and changing them all the time, that's also a systems problem. The vision can be strong and the preaching can be good, but it might be the systems holding you back.

The problems we were facing in our young and growing church were systems problems.

So eighteen months in, we went to work.

I made a list of every system that needed to exist in our organization—from how we hired and interviewed people, to how a service got planned, to how the truck was loaded. We wrote them all down. Thankfully, there were people on our team who were gifted in this area. They were more organized than I was, and without their help we never would have gotten anywhere.

It took us months and several meetings, but eventually we wrote down every system in our church. We began to implement these systems, and they revolutionized the day-to-day operations of our church. People problems seemed to go away because our people knew what we expected of them. Volunteers knew what they were responsible for and who to call in case they needed something. Meetings took shape because we knew the goal and the desired result.

YOUR BIGGEST PROBLEM IS FREE TO FIX

Most of the systems and strategies in this book are free to implement. In other words, you don't have to do a capital campaign or spend a lot of money to dramatically improve your ministry. I'm not going to propose you hire a branding consultant or build a new auditorium in order to reach new people. The solutions here will be far less invasive but potentially just as impactful. Creating healthy systems won't break the bank.

In reality, money won't solve the deepest problems in your church. If your church isn't healthy, a bigger budget won't change that. If your church isn't friendly toward outsiders, a bigger auditorium won't fix that. Just like with people, money will only make you more of who you already are.

God has given us resources and people, and He will only give us more to the degree we are faithful. So instead of worrying about what we don't have, let's focus our attention on effectively leading and stewarding what God has already put in our care.

SYSTEMS AND THE HOLY SPIRIT

The ideas, strategies, and tools I'm going to discuss in this book do not negate the power of the Holy Spirit. God can do anything He wants to do. He certainly doesn't need a super-organized pastor to reach people.

But leadership is a stewardship issue.

If God has called you to pastor a congregation or work with a local church, you're called to work at it wholeheartedly, "as working for the Lord and not for man." God can speak through a donkey, but He can also speak through a preacher who is "rightly dividing the Word of Truth."

Sadly, too many leaders blame the Holy Spirit for their lack of thought, planning, or hard work. Relying on the Holy Spirit does not negate the need for thoughtful planning. As you've undoubtedly experienced, when you're organized, you often give the Holy Spirit *more* time and space to work. Maybe this isn't true for you, but I'm not that smart. So if proper planning gives God more time to work on me, that's a good thing.

Proverbs 21:31 says, "The horse is made ready for the day of battle, but victory rests with the LORD." God certainly does His part, but we've got preparation work to do as well. We desperately need the Holy Spirit, but most of us could also use some good systems.

Creating these systems won't only make you more efficient, as if the goal is to work the least amount of hours as possible. It makes you more effective. And because the mission of the church is to make disciples, effectiveness has eternal implications.

HOW THIS BOOK IS ORGANIZED

This book is divided into three sections, each containing a number of small chapters.

> » In Section 1, we will talk about calendars and planning. Many of the steps in this book are built on these fundamental ideas.

> » In Section 2, we will talk about organizing and aligning your leaders. You'll find helpful steps whether you have a large staff or a small team, or whether your staff consists of full-time employees or mostly volunteers.

> » In Section 3, we will turn our attention to communication, both internal and external. You'll see how many of these steps intersect with the calendar.

Most chapters contain one big principle and one specific homework assignment. If you don't like homework, you can think of them as action steps. My intention was to keep the theory to a minimum and get right to the implementation. Some of the action steps can be completed relatively quickly, but some will require a little longer.

Some you will be able to do by yourself, while others will require you to assemble a task force.

While you can certainly read the book in a handful of sittings, it's designed to be processed one chapter at a time. The idea isn't to read the book, but to implement the book. So read a chapter and then implement what you learn. It's far better to actually organize one or two areas of your church than to read about organizing all of them.

Throughout the book, I will reference documents and templates. Many of these are available at churchfuel.com. While you can start from scratch, I've found that it's often better to start with an example and customize it for your setting. Not only can you be more efficient with your time, you'll be able to build and improve upon existing ideas, creating a win/win.

The mission of the church matters so let's give it our best and let's get to work. Let's make sure the quality of our systems match the importance of our mission.

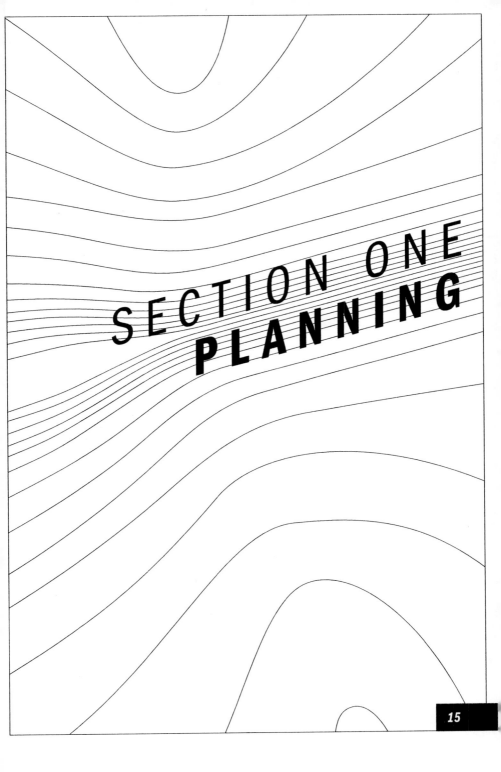

SECTION ONE
PLANNING

- 1 -

CREATE AN ANNUAL CALENDAR

If you don't know where you are going,
you might wind up somewhere else.

- Yogi Berra -

There's a secret weapon when it comes to organizing your church.

It's not fancy and it requires no numbers. This particular tool has been around for thousands of years and it has helped countless of people, families, and organizations. The solution I'm going to propose in this chapter might sound like a passionate sermon that ends with a challenge for people to read the Bible. Everybody knows that, but few people do it.

I'm talking about a calendar.

Hunters used calendars to know when wild game would migrate south. Farmers used them to know when to plant their corn. The ancient Jews used them to mark the date of Pentecost or celebrate the beginning of the year of Jubilee.

Without calendars, we wouldn't know when the football season starts, when to set our clocks forward an hour, or when to blow up millions of dollars of fireworks on the 4th of July.

A simple calendar is one of the most powerful tools you can use to organize your church.

I'm going to talk about four different calendars your church should have, but I'll begin with the most important one, which I simply call an annual calendar.

An annual calendar isn't a calendar for *this* year...it's a calendar for *every* year. It's an at-a-glance overview of your entire year. And it's one of the most important things you can create for your church.

> » What happens in your church in January...*every* January?
>
> » What do you do in the summer...*every* summer?
>
> » How do you kick off the fall...*every* fall?
>
> » What do you do during the Christmas season...*every* Christmas season?

I'm going to tell you how, but first, let me tell you why you need an annual calendar.

1. Success is best measured over time. Doing something once might not give you a true indicator of success for your organization. First year churches and organizations shouldn't put too much stock into first year numbers, because they aren't real. You've got to measure things over a longer time period.

2. Life has a natural rhythm. Whether it's the back to school season, the Christmas holidays, or the early emergence of spring, life has a season just like the weather. You'd be wise to understand the seasons of your industry and plan accordingly. Great leaders don't just react to the current season, but intentionally build a calendar knowing how to connect the dots. People in your organization or community understand the rhythm or life, so stop trying to fight it.

3. There is power in tradition. When it comes to organizations, traditionalism is bad but tradition is good. When you do some of the same things year after year, you build a story. "Ladies and gentlemen...start your engines"—that's a tradition. So are Christmas Eve family candlelight services, and the staff Olympics. Annual picnics, big events, and company retreats can go a long way towards building a culture. Don't be so quick to discount the meaning of tradition, and remember that not all traditions are sacred cows. Not only should you appreciate traditions, you should leverage them. In the quest to be innovative and relevant, don't cast aside something valuable.

4. Repetition leads to improvement. When you do something once, you don't really know if it worked. For example, after a near disastrous Easter outreach event, our entire team would have supported the idea of wiping it from the church calendar forevermore. But after a few evaluation meetings, we decided some simple adjustments would make it more effective. I committed to host the large-scale event one more time before making the final decision. The following year, attendance was lower but the event went smoother. We worked out the kinks and, in the end, the event lasted a total of five years. Had we pulled the plug after the initial flop, we wouldn't have been able to gauge its true effectiveness.

5. Patterns will keep things from sneaking up on you. When people say, "That just snuck up on me," they generally mean, "I'm disorganized and wasn't paying attention." So stop reacting to whatever is current and start planning in bulk. Plan the year in advance, and know when it's time to start working on something. When you plan an annual calendar, you'll know what's going on in June and July. And after a few seasons, advance planning will become second nature.

6. A calendar will keep you from competing with yourself.
Churches are among the worst culprits when it comes to internal competition. It's routine for people to be encouraged to get in a small group, sign up for a mission trip, bring in school supplies, set up online giving, and volunteer in their kid's class, all on one Sunday. What is your church emphasizing in the month of October? Are there strategic times for an emphasis on groups where other ministries can chill out on the public communication? When you get your entire team in the room and work on the big picture calendar, you'll stop stepping on each other's toes and stop confusing your people with multiple action steps.

IT'S EVEN MORE IMPORTANT TO PLAN THE ORDINARY

When it comes to planning and creating calendars, the more ordinary the ministry the more important it is to plan properly. In the church world, the regular programs and ministries often get pushed off the plate because of special events. These "now" events take us away from the everyday ministries.

Think back to your last few weeks. How much time did you spend planning or working on something out of the ordinary compared to your regular programs and ministries? It's tough to plan the normal stuff because we feel like we've got a handle on it all. But in reality, the regular stuff needs focus.

I'm convinced planning will solve (or at least dramatically help) most problems in the church. You may *want* to get people into small groups, but what's your plan and when are you emphasizing it? You may *want* to get better when it comes to stewardship, but when are you planning to talk about money? Carving out time on your annual calendar for these ordinary things is one of the biggest keys to success.

> » When are you launching groups? Not this next time, but every time.

> » When are you preaching on money and tying it to a next-step class or group? That needs to happen every year.

> » When are you recruiting volunteers and connecting them to existing teams? If you're only responding to crisis needs and not putting this on your annual calendar, the pressure will return time and time again.

HOW TO CREATE AN ANNUAL CALENDAR

Now that you understand a little bit of the power when it comes to the annual calendar, let's talk about how to create one. We'll come back to this a few times throughout this book, but there's no reason why you can't start on the beta version right away.

Step 1: Do your homework.

Start by creating a simple spreadsheet. You can use Excel, Google or even a legal pad and a pencil. Put the months of the year in rows across the top. Then list categories down the left side. Examples of categories might be Preaching, Children's Ministry, Students, Discipleship, Staff or Special Events.

Then go ahead and fill in what you know. If your church always does a homecoming service in November, type it in the appropriate cell. If a Junior High retreat happens each spring, write it down. Vacation Bible School, Small Group Sunday, the Volunteer Fair... write down everything that happens on an annual basis. There will surely be events that happen only once in the life of your church and that's okay. Your mission is to write down the things that happen every year.

You're going to move, edit, add, and delete in the next step. You're going to involve other people, too, but for now your job is to get everything out of your head and onto your screen.

	January	February	March	April	May	June
Financial	Send Annual Contribution Statement	Financial Peace University		Send Quarterly Contribution Statement	Online Giving Campaign	
Volunteers		Leadership Summit	Thank You Week		Leadership Summit	Strategic Service Message
Worship Service						God at the Movies
Special Events		Business Summit		Easter Egg Hunt		
Discipleship	Small Group Kickoff					
Family Ministry			Junior High Retreat			Vacation Bible School
Internal	Quarterly Retreat	Review Staff Job Descriptions	Quarterly Retreat			Quarterly Retreat

Figure 1. A Microsoft Excel Version of an annual calendar. Visit churchfuel.com/streamline to download this template for free.

Step 2: Spend half a day with all of your staff or key ministry leaders.

The best way to lock down your annual calendar is to get the majority of the principle leaders in one room and work on it together. You can create this on your own, but I've found that systems created alone are typically followed alone. The more you involve other people in the process, the more excited they'll be about the result.

Creating an annual church calendar is a great way to create conversations and build buy-in among all of your leaders. Frankly, you need to have some discussions about what to do and when. If the month of June gets loaded with too many activities, you need to lead the charge to simplify and rearrange. Your church is not a collection of ministries held together by a common thread. It's the body of Christ. Every ministry affects every other ministry.

This is why your annual calendar discussion needs representatives from each ministry. You can even involve volunteer leaders in this meeting. Putting all the key players in the room gives you the widest possible perspective.

Argue, debate, and discuss based on the calendar. You're not debating the merits of each ministry or program (we're going to get to that later in the book). You're looking factually at the events and activities central to the life of your church. Like a puzzle, your goal is to make everything fit together for one great purpose.

It may take a while, but imagine the synergy that will come from all of your key leaders having a general framework about what to do. Imagine walking away from this meeting with a big picture understanding of a year in the life of your church.

One of the biggest benefits from creating an annual calendar is teamwork. With every conversation and every change, you're tearing down the ministry silos and working toward a comprehensive calendar. Through a very tangible process, ministry leaders see there's more at stake than the ministry they lead.

ACTION STEP

Download the annual calendar template from churchfuel.com/streamline and start documenting what happens in your church every year.

- 2 -

PLAN YOUR PREACHING

The secret of all victory lies in the organization of the non-obvious.

- Marcus Aurelius

As we saw in the last chapter, stepping back and looking at your year as a whole can have a dramatic effect on your ministry. But there's another type of calendar you need: a preaching calendar.

A preaching calendar is simply a plan of *when* you're going to preach about *what*. Like your annual calendar, it's a big picture look at your entire year. God should lead you to your topics, but write them down on a preaching calendar.

The idea of a preaching calendar makes sense to a lot of pastors, but there's still a lot of confusion on the topic. Some people believe the very idea of a preaching calendar cannot co-exist with the Holy Spirit. Spirit-led preaching, they say, can't be confined to a spreadsheet. "How can you know what God wants to say to the church three months in advance?" they ask.

Some pastors inherited or learned a preparation system that doesn't work well. On Monday, they head into the study and work on the upcoming message. The next week, they do it all over again. They have little time to think about future sermon topics when this week's message is looming.

Still, there are more pastors who would love the *ideas* of a preaching calendar, but aren't wired to create (or to live with) such a document. They are passionate and responsive, and long-term plans don't combine well with their personality.

But the benefits of a thoughtful, Bible-based preaching calendar far outweigh those concerns. What you will get, and more importantly, what your church will experience by having a solid preaching plan, is a compelling reason to implement the steps I'm going to share in this chapter.

BENEFITS OF A PREACHING CALENDAR

So let's talk about some of the benefits of a preaching calendar. Why should you do the hard work to create this document?

1. You have more time to study.

D. Martyn Lloyd-Jones wrote, "To me, the work of preaching is the highest and the greatest and the most glorious calling to which anyone can ever be called....I would say without any hesitation that the most urgent need in the Christian Church today is true preaching."

Today, there is much that a pastor must do. In addition to teaching, we often counsel, meet, and lead. We should be in the business of developing relationships with those who don't know Christ. But in the midst of all our duties and responsibilities, we must not forget that it's the weekly sermon that deserves our focus.

If preparing your message during the week was the only thing on your job description, you'd deliver brilliant messages every Sunday. I admire the preachers who can spend 20-30 hours a week in their study, studying the text and preparing their message. Most preachers don't have that luxury. I've coached preachers who said their biggest issue was finding the time to prepare their sermon.

In this chapter, I can't help you to find more time. We've all got the same number of hours in the day. But I can help you be far more effective with those hours.

Putting more time between selecting your topic and delivering your message works in the same way as working more hours on a particular sermon. Spreading out your preparation time is more effective than cramming your prep into a solid block of hours. Your preparation time will be more effective and your sermons will be better if you spend more time on them. I'm not talking about the number of hours spent writing them, I'm talking about the overall length of time that a subject is on your mind and heart.

When you know what passages you're covering, and what topics you're addressing in the future, you can keep your antenna up for ideas and insights. God speaks to you during your personal Bible reading time. You may see a news article and realize it's a sermon illustration. Life happens and it makes your upcoming sermon richer.

If you know your topics, you can capture all of this and work it into your messages.

Planning doesn't necessarily give God more time to speak to you (He can speak whenever He wants). It gives *you* more time to listen to God. I don't know why it took me so long to realize this, but it's been one of the biggest realizations in my church leadership career. Planning is not for God's benefit, it's for ours! God can show up whenever and wherever he wants and He is not limited by our plans and ideas. He doesn't need our plans, but we need them. God doesn't need a schedule or a calendar, but we do.

When you have a longer runway with your sermon topic, you have more time to dive deeper into sermon preparation. For example, you can read books instead of blogs. If you have an upcoming series on the life of Christ, you can order several books and read. If it's Monday and you haven't started any of your work, it's too easy to head to the internet. The quality of work there is dramatically different.

When you have a longer runway, you can search the Scriptures instead of scanning podcasts. Listening to well-known preachers is fine, but it's a poor substitute for real sermon prep. A sermon calendar will give you more time to hear from God

2. You can involve others.

I love the word *arguably*. You can insert this word into any controversial sentence and immediately temper the emotion.

- » I am *arguably* the funniest person in the world.

- » Skinny Jeans are *arguably* the worst fashion trend ever.

- » The Dallas Cowboys are *arguably* the most overrated team in the NFL.

You can't argue with these statements because I included the word *arguably*. It's as if I'm almost willing to make a bold statement, but I want to cover all of my bases.

Well, preaching is arguably the most important element in any church service. Even if you disagree with that bold statement, you'd have to agree that it's really important.

So why would you choose to hunker down in your office and keep wise, Godly people who could offer incredible insight at arm's length? What if you found a way to involve other people in your message prep process?

You can do this, but only if you know where you're going. Planning a message calendar gives you the time to involve the appropriate people at the appropriate times. One of the biggest reasons to create a long-term preaching plan is the ability to involve other people in the sermon prep process.

3. You can be more creative.

You might be able to exegete and outline the text and write a good sermon in a week. But if there are other people involved in your service, they will benefit from more time.

Let's take the worship leader or the music director, for example. Maybe there are some new songs that fit with a series or a book of the Bible. With enough time, your worship team could learn these songs and integrate them into a service. Without a thorough plan, they might select good songs and pull them off with a certain degree of quality. However, with time on their side, they may be able to do an even better job and really connect the songs to the theme of the message.

On more than one occasion, I've wanted a prop or display to make the message come alive. Time was the critical factor for being able to execute some of these ideas. Whether it's a video, props, announcements, or other elements, there's incredible power when all of the service elements work together.

4. Your preaching will be more diverse.

A thoughtful preaching calendar will help ensure you're talking about the most important topics. But it will also force you to adopt a broader approach to selecting topics.

We all naturally gravitate to our favorite topics and passages. When I was in college, I remember a preacher who figured out how to make every sermon about the book of Revelation. Clearly, he was interested in the end times. If he could have it his way, every sermon would be about this topic.

A preaching calendar will force you to address uncomfortable topics. If you're a big believer in grace and second chances, your calendar should force you to wrestle with the issues of law and justice. It will stretch you as a preacher and facilitate the preaching of the whole counsel of God's Word.

THE PREACHING CALENDAR
AND THE HOLY SPIRIT

Just as systems and the Holy Spirit can go together, a preaching calendar and the Holy Spirit can work in tandem.

If your view of God limits God to speaking at the last minute, I'd say your view of God is too small. The same God who speaks on Saturday night can speak three months in advance. The same inspiration that hits on a Thursday can hit during a planning meeting.

Your preaching plan isn't for God's benefit...it's for yours.

HOW TO CREATE A PREACHING CALENDAR

The benefits of a preaching calendar far outweigh the amount of work it takes to create and live by it. Maybe you're ready to give it a try. Let's talk about how to actually create this preaching plan.

You can hunker down in your office with a legal pad or an Excel spreadsheet, taking all of those ideas you've scribbled in notebooks and collected from other preachers and start filling in the blanks.

But there's a better way.

You have the opportunity to involve other people in this important process, and as a result, you'll end up with a far better preaching plan. I recommend that you organize a sermon planning retreat.

This retreat should last for one to two days and involve three to seven people. Those aren't the perfect numbers, but I've found they work well for most churches. If you pull some people together for a day or two, you can create a really solid preaching plan for the next 12 months.

A sermon planning retreat, lasting from one to two days and

involving three to seven people, is the best way to create a teaching calendar for the next 12 months. Here's a three-step process to plan your planning retreat.

Step One: Schedule and Invite

Go ahead and choose a date, time, and place. Then put it on the calendar. You can do this right now. October would be a great month, but if October is too far away, go ahead and schedule one and work on the next six months.

Once you pick the best time of the year for this sermon planning retreat, you can put it on your annual calendar. This first retreat will be helpful, but it will be even better the second time. This is one of those events that should show up on the annual calendar and become a consistent part of your ministry.

Who should you invite to a sermon planning retreat? Here are a few suggestions:

» **Creative Arts Staff or Worship Leaders.** People involved in service planning are in a great position to offer incredible insight into this process.

» **Other teachers and leaders in your church**. If you're working to develop another preacher or communicator, there's nothing better than bringing them into the sermon planning process.

» **Another pastor from another church.** This might be a new idea for you, but there might be a pastor in your community or network who understands the value of this process.

» **Elders or Deacons.** Spiritual leaders in your church will often have great insight into what should be preached from the pulpit.

» **Men and Women.** Make sure your group is diverse and doesn't represent just one segment of your church. It's entirely possible your congregation is made up of more women than men, so it's smart to make sure you're factoring that into your planning.

Step Two: Pray and Prepare

Once your event is scheduled and you've invited the right participants, it's time to do some pre-planning.

Before you get people together to start brainstorming, pray and connect with God. "God, what do you want me to say to your church?" is a prayer that you must continually pray. But you should spend some focused time asking this question as you get close to your planning retreat.

After taking time to pray and listen to God, and after reviewing information from your church, make a list of your teaching priorities. This is essentially a prayerful mind-dump, where you'll list all of the topics you believe God wants you to cover in the next year. You'll arrange this on the calendar later. Your goal here is to get your thoughts down on paper.

Your list might look something like this:

» Leveraging your gifts and talents by volunteering twice a year

» Becoming a generous giver. A whole series on generosity

» Connecting with the Biblical community in a small group. Need this message twice a year as we launch small groups

» Begin reading the Bible. Maybe in conjunction with a church-wide reading plan we create

» The big picture vision of our church. A good message for our 10 year anniversary service

» Ephesians belief and behavior. God has really been speaking to me about how our activity must be driven by our identity.

You might also find a congregational survey helpful.

A simple survey like this is a great way to collect the spiritual habits or musical tastes of your congregation. It's also a way of ensuring that you're answering questions that people are actually asking.

Whether you reserve a few minutes to complete a survey during the worship service, or conduct an online version, ask people what they're struggling with and what they want to learn. Allow them to rank several topics and give them an opportunity to share their own thoughts.

As you schedule your survey, you might find it helpful to conduct it for two weeks in a row in order to catch most of your regular attenders.

The final part of the preparation process involves sending everything to the people attending your retreat. It's not enough to prepare yourself. You've got to prepare the entire team. If everyone coming on your retreat is already on the same page, you'll really maximize your time and be more effective. Everyone should have the following items and information *before* they come on the retreat:

- » **The church annual calendar with all the important dates and planned activities.** We talked about that in Chapter 1. Your preaching calendar should support the church calendar, not compete with it.

- » **Your teaching priorities.** They need to know what God has said to you, the leader of the church.

- » **The public school or community calendar.** It's smart to know what's happening in your community.

- » **Survey results.** Let everyone know what the congregation said on the survey.

Send this to everyone in advance and ask them to prayerfully process it all. By doing this hard work and preparing your team, you're showing them how important this retreat is to the life and health of the church.

Step Three: Execute the Retreat

Once everyone knows what to expect and what's at stake, it's time to execute your retreat.

The best retreats are away from the office and last for at least one night. There's something refreshing about getting away from it all and changing your perspective. Mark Batterson says breakthrough sometimes comes when you have a "change of pace and a change of place."

The goal here isn't leadership development or team building, though some of that will undoubtedly happen. In a way, this is like a SWAT team, assembled for one specific purpose. The mission and the result should be very clear to everyone. The goal of the sermon planning retreat is to create a preaching plan, putting all of the information into a spreadsheet that looks something like this:

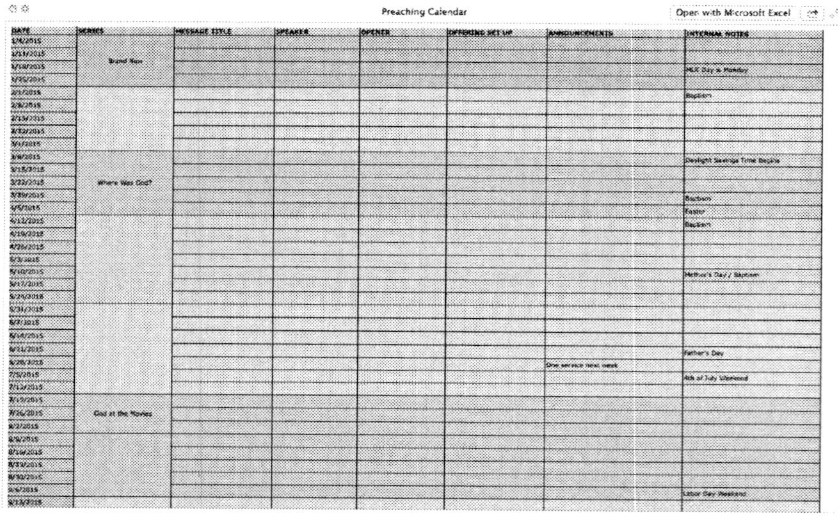

Figure 2 – An Excel Version of a Preaching Calendar. You can download this template for free at churchfuel.com/streamline.

Once you put the right people in the right room and focus on the right objective, the results tend to occur naturally. You can schedule your retreat in a way that works well for you, but I suggest a macro approach at first that moves at a swift pace toward specifics. Something like this might work well:

1. **Start big.** Figure out how many teaching series' you need in the calendar year and talk about the overall focus of each series. You don't have to know how many weeks or where it fits on the calendar yet.

2. **Flesh it out.** Once you know the series and major topics, you can get into specific texts or topics. For example, if you're doing a marriage and family series in October, you can talk about what topics you want to cover during that series and place them all on the calendar.

3. ***Really* flesh it out.** Start putting topics on the spreadsheet. It's okay to throw out creative ideas here, too. Don't chase the rabbit for too long, but give people some space to dream.

Imagine how you will feel knowing your preaching plan for the next 12 months. Let's say you have to dial this back and can only create a plan for the next six months. You're still going to feel great, and your sermon prep will immediately improve.

ACTION STEP

Visit churchfuel.com/streamline and download the Preaching Calendar template. Customize it for what you already know. Then schedule a planning retreat where you'll fill in the rest of the details.

- 3 -

BUILD YOUR WEEKEND COMMUNICATION CALENDAR

A goal without a plan is just a wish.
- Antoine de Saint-Exupery -

Have you ever said something like this? *Man, that event snuck up on me.*

It seems like programs and events continually sneak up on church leaders. But events and programs can't sneak. They aren't alive. They're words on a calendar, totally incapable of physical actions such as sneaking.

People sneak. Cats sneak. But inanimate programs and events don't have the ability to sneak. Don't blame the event for the fact you weren't paying proper attention to the date. The fact that an event snuck up on you is all about you.

The sneak-up effect is the result of poor planning. That's why a detailed calendar is so effective. A properly developed church calendar doesn't only list events; it tells you when to start planning and when to communicate.

We're three chapters into this book, and all three chapters have been about calendars so far. We're going to get to other stuff later in the book. We're going to talk about ministries, and reaching guests, and working with a staff. But, many of those things will come back to the very basic idea of the church calendar. I'm going to harp on about it a little more because it really does matter.

There's so much potential to organize and align with a tool as simple as a calendar. That's why it's one of the most important planning tools in your church. It's the closest thing you have to a silver bullet.

By now, you should have two calendars. The annual calendar doesn't have dates—it's an annual snapshot of everything that happens in your church every year. The preaching calendar is a week-by-week look at your sermon topics. With both of these calendars in hand, we're going to build on them.

Now it's time to get insanely practical and build a communication calendar.

THE MYTH OF THE BUSY SEASON

You know that "busy season" you feel like your church is in? The sad reality for most churches is that season never changes. The New Year becomes Easter, which leads right into Mother's Day. Summer should be a little more relaxed, but there's VBS and youth camp and more activities than you first realized. Before you know it, you're in the middle of the Fall growth season which runs non-stop into the Holiday season. You roll from one busy season right into the next one, without much pause for reflection, evaluation, or rest.

There are so many programs, ministries, and special events vying for communication in your church. The Sunday handout, weekend announcements, email newsletter, and website become a cluttered mess. Before you know it, your handouts and stage announcements are muddied with mixed messages.

When your church is busy it means your communication is confusing. There's simply too much to announce. There are too many things to say.

Your busy church calendar leads to a confusing message for your people. They don't know what's most important and they can't decide what to attend or where to serve.

Have you played the game of "What announcement are we going to cut this weekend?" You have five announcements to make but you only have time to focus on three. So you decide which ones can wait until next week, or you try and figure out who will get the least mad for being left out.

Have you ever been approached right before the service by a volunteer or staff member with a "Hey, don't forget to announce" statement?

> » *Hey pastor, can you please announce that the women's Bible study starts this week?*
>
> » *Remind people to drop off diapers for the diaper drive.*
>
> » *Don't forget to mention the student camp deadline.*

You don't want to hurt anyone's feelings so you give it a half-hearted mention during the welcome or a quick "by the way" at the beginning of the message. You and I both know that these announcements may make a staff member feel better but they rarely work. It's well-intentioned white noise.

When people hear too many announcements, they don't pay attention to any of them. Let's say you spend thirty seconds each on five announcements. That's two and a half minutes with five different focuses. At the end of the service, it's likely people won't remember any of them.

What if you took those two and a half minutes and focused on just one thing? In addition to sharing the information (which is all you had time to do in the example above), you also talk about the benefits people will get from attending. You may share a story of someone who was impacted by this activity in the past. Or you could show a video. You're communicating less, but you're really communicating more.

Yes, this means those other four things won't get announced. But let's face it...nobody was paying attention to them anyway. You've just redeemed this time and made it far more valuable for everyone involved.

If you're a leader, communication is like money in the bank. You have to spend it wisely. Ask people to do too much and they won't do anything at all. Focus those announcements by using multiple channels and you'll be far more successful.

That's why it's time to take your annual calendar and your weekend communication calendar and decide in advance how to handle announcements.

You might already have a calendar, but do you have a communication calendar?

> » Most church calendars list the dates of VBS in the summer. A communication calendar includes key decisions and communication milestones. You're not just planning the event, you're planning when you're going to talk about the event.

> » Most church calendars list the dates for Student Ministry Camp. A communication calendar aligns the opening day of sign ups with the student pastor preaching in the weekend services.

> » Most church calendars have some type of Stewardship Sunday or generosity emphasis. A communication calendar includes details on the kickoff of Financial Peace University, plus the dates for sending contribution statements and emphasizing online giving.

It's not enough to plan the event. You must also plan your communication about the event. Your communication calendar should let you know when to talk about what. A lot of churches put programs and events on the calendar but very few take the time to write down all of the communication plans and ensure those plans don't step on the toes of other ministries.

When you're thinking through your communication plan, here are some questions to consider:

1. When do sign ups begin and when is the deadline to sign up?
2. When is the group planning meeting for that regular event?

3. When does the information get *featured* in the bulletin and on the website?
4. When do we focus on social media engagement?
5. When do we send targeted emails?
6. When do we start recruiting volunteers?
7. When do we announce in the service?

In *Church Unique*, Will Mancini shares a powerful illustration about vision alignment, which also applies to communication.

Imagine six people gathered around a large metal ring. At the count of three, each person pulls on the ring in their direction. Lots of force is exerted, but that ring doesn't move. There's a whole lot of trying but very little motion. Now imagine all six of those individuals coming to one side of the ring. On the count of three, they all pull in one direction. That ring is moving, and it's moving fast. That's the power of focus and alignment.

I'm telling you, there is power in alignment. But alignment won't come naturally. You have to fight for it.

Many church programs and events never reach their full potential because there is little focus and alignment on the communication plan. An announcement here and an email there are not enough to get the attention of people in the church who are used to hearing a dozen things at a time.

When you build a full communication calendar, it allows you to place more emphasis on fewer things. If you're promoting student camp, you can focus your entire church messaging around that one idea for a set period of time. The video in the service, midweek email blast to the database, and Facebook posts will all work together. You could even align the offering setup (more on that in just a minute).

Listen carefully, because the following is of the most important communication lessons I've learned in 20 years of working with churches. We don't need to spend less time announcing things; we need to spend more time announcing fewer things.

Spend more time on fewer things. Decide which things really matter and communicate *more*. Tell stories. Shoot videos. Print flyers. Use all the resources at your disposal. But not on everything, only on the main things.

So let's get practical. How do you build a communication calendar?

Start with the very same spreadsheet you use for your preaching calendar. This is where you record the basic details about your teaching. You might have columns and rows to track the following:

- » Series Title

- » Message Title

- » Speaker

- » Bottom Line from the Message

- » Worship Leader

That's a great start. Now let's add some further columns and more detailed information that will help us focus our communication on the most important things. Specifically, add two more columns and plan two more things to communicate each week.

With your annual calendar in mind and your preaching calendar in hand, go ahead and decide what will get stage time in your service. Your regular programs and ministries need to be announced, so give them enough time and space. In my experience with helping churches with their communication, I've found that most people spend their time announcing the special stuff and not the regular stuff. It's the regular programs and ministries that make the most difference in the life of the church.

You need to talk about the things that happen in your church on a regular basis. Your regular ministries get the most money in your budget and most of your focus throughout the week. They also need the most announcement time in your service.

Have you seen that time management example with the big rocks, pebbles, and sand? Someone fills a jar with sand, then pebbles, and then tries to add rocks. Because the jar is full, the rocks don't fit. Then he reverses the process, filling the jar with the big rocks, then adding the pebbles and finally the sand. Everything fits because he put the big rocks in first. This is a great example of doing the most important things first, but it's also true when it comes to communication. When you're planning your services you need to devote enough time to talk about the "big rocks." If you fill the time with pebbles and sand, you won't leave enough time to talk about what matters most.

So go ahead and decide on these "big rocks." Decide how many weeks you're going to talk about what's happening with the weekly children's ministry or student ministry. Decide when to talk about small groups or regular discipleship opportunities.

WHEN TO TALK ABOUT WHAT

Next, assign time to the big events you do on an annual basis. Those special events on the calendar need enough time and space to work. Let me give you some examples of how to build this out.

If you've decided to emphasize small groups in September, a good preaching calendar might have you preach on the importance of small groups a couple of Sundays before groups begin. On that same Sunday, you might have a testimony from someone who was skeptical to join a group but decided to jump in anyway. The announcements that day might focus on the sign up process. Do you see how all this works together?

On this Sunday, the entire service points to one clear, compelling, and very important action step.

The month of May is a great time to talk about generosity and specifically challenge people to set up reoccurring donations on your church website. You can go ahead and decide to talk about this for three weeks in a row. One week you could show a screencast of how easy it is to do. The next week you could ask people to turn in a card to express interest in giving online. The third week you could share a generosity story in conjunction with an announcement. Throughout this process you could email similar information to your congregation and promote social media posts specifically to your church members.

Every year, you have 52 opportunities to communicate next steps. Those are important moments and need to be filled with vision, stories, and creativity. By deciding what to communicate in advance, you claim the communication space for what you determine to be the most important. If you limit yourself to two announcements each Sunday, that's 104 points of emphasis. Spend them wisely.

And back them up with email support, direct mail support, social media posts, and more. Use all of the communication assets at your disposal. Align them for maximum effectiveness. If you do all of this, you'll end up spending the same amount of time communicating but you'll see a much greater impact for your efforts.

ACTION STEP

Decide when to start planning and when to start announcing the events that are already on your calendar. Go ahead and write these dates down.

- 4 -

PUT EVERYTHING ON A MASTER CALENDAR

In preparing for battle I have always found that plans are useless, but planning is indispensable.

– Dwight D. Eisenhower

A few years ago, I created a bunch of documents to help churches get organized. All in all, it was more than 120 Word documents, Excel spreadsheets, and flow charts. I created these because we needed them in our own church, but I quickly learned that other churches needed them too.

So I zipped them together and put them on a website. I called this downloadable resource *Docs and Forms*.

With one click, pastors and church planters had access to tons of documents to help organize their church. Thousands of pastors have downloaded these resources. The name might not have been creative, but the product was helpful.

If you've followed each of the steps we've talked about in this book, you have three calendars. You have an annual calendar that provides an overall framework for the year. You have a Preaching Calendar to guide the content of your sermons and church services. And you've got a Communication Calendar so you know when to talk about what.

Now it's time to put all of your information in one place. I'm going to call this *The Master Calendar*. I know it's not very creative, but at least it's clear.

All three of these calendars will help you organize critical areas in your church, but when you synchronize everything into one document, it's like magic.

If you're a Lord of the Rings fan, you've read this inscription about the one ring to rule them all:

> *Eleven rings for the Eleven-kings under the sky*
> *Seven for the Dwarf-lords in their halls of stone*
> *Nine for Mortal Men doomed to die,*
> *One for the Dark Lord on his dark throne*
> *In the Land of Mordor where the Shadows lie.*
> *One Ring to rule them all*
> *One Ring to find them*
> *One Ring to bring them all and in the darkness bind them.*

In *The Hobbit*, Bilbo found the ring in Gollum's cave and fought to get it home to the Shire. In the Lord of the Rings trilogy, Frodo and the Fellowship went on a dangerous quest to destroy it, ending the rule of Sauron once and for all. This one ring held the power.

Hopefully you see where I'm going with this nerdy example. You need one calendar to rule them all. You must create one document that brings together all of the important information. The leaders in your church need one master calendar that combines events with sermons and communication.

How do you create it? What tool do you use? I can tell you what

I'd do, but this is one of those times where you simply need to pick something that works and go with it. Too many times we're tempted by new technology. Just lock down an online solution and go with it. End your search for the perfect calendar and use the one you already have.

I recommend iCal or Google Calendar. These solutions allow you to share the master calendar with everyone on your staff and your key volunteers. You can give access to the people that need it and they can view it on their computers and devices. But pick something that works for you and put *all* of your master calendar stuff in one place.

Here are some things that should go on your Master Calendar:

» Special events

» Volunteer training or appreciation events

» Small group sign ups

» Sign up periods

» Staff Review Week

» Staff retreats or staff training

» Mission trips and local service opportunities

» Conferences that you and your team will attend

» Baptism

» Community events

» Direct mail and advertising campaigns

» Contribution statements mailed

» Vacations

Your master calendar should contain all of your regular programs and ministries, as well as your special events. Bring together your preaching calendar and your communication calendar and put all of your information in one place.

SOME OTHER BEST PRACTICES:

1. Appoint one person to be the master of the master calendar.

While you can share your calendar with lots of people, appointing too many managers is a recipe for disaster. You need a Frodo— one person entrusted with managing, updating, and ensuring the accuracy of your master calendar. This one person can pull in information from your teaching calendar and make changes (because yes, things will change). The keeper of the calendar can be tasked with ensuring everything is accurate and up-to-date.

2. Create a physical calendar and keep it in a common area in your office.

I love the ease of accessing digital information. It's so easy to share calendars and invites. But I also love seeing the entire year hanging on a wall. That's why I personally use a giant wall calendar. It's so useful for planning but also visualizing. Wouldn't it be great to have an accurate calendar hanging on the wall in your office?

You can get a wall calendar from any office store or you can order one from Amazon.com. But I wanted to make something that's prettier and more efficient, so I created The Church Calendar.

It's 29" x 36" and beautifully designed. The year is broken into four quarters (you'll see why that matters a little later in this book).

Key holidays and dates for your church are pre-printed, but there's lots of space for you to add your own events. You can get it at churchfuel.com/calendar.

3. Create an online version and make sure everyone has access.

While it's great to have a physical calendar in a common area, you should also create a digital version of your master calendar and share it with staff and leaders. Frodo might manage it all, but all of the Hobbits need access. The elves and dwarves, too. You could use Google or Basecamp or any number of online tools for this.

4. Review your calendar regularly.

One of the biggest benefits of having an accurate calendar that effectively lays out the future is that you can talk about this in your meetings. You can keep all of the communication in front of your team during weekly meetings because all of this information is in one place. We used to end every one of our team meetings by having someone walk through the next several weeks of the calendar. Since all the hard work and decisions were already made, this was quick communication to ensure alignment.

A calendar is one of the simplest but most powerful resources to help you keep your ministry moving in the right direction. It solves a myriad of problems and it's virtually free to use.

ACTION STEP

Get a wall calendar and fill it up with your dates for the year.
Not a digital calendar or a shared Google calendar,
but an old-school, hang-on-the-wall variety.

54

- 5 -

EVALUATE YOUR REGULAR PROGRAMS

The first responsibility of a leader is to define reality.

- Max De Pree -

A lot of churches are *tired*.

The pastors and leaders are tired because they have been plowing the field for so long. Volunteers are tired because they have been working week after week for years and years.

And even the ministries themselves sometimes seem tired. It's the same thing, week after week, season after season.

The Apostle Paul said we should run with purpose, not wandering aimlessly or beating the air. But let's be honest, sometimes ministry feels like we're beating the air. We move from program to program or problem to problem and we feel like we're never making progress. What used to work in the past (or what works for other people) doesn't seem to make a difference. You try new things but get the same old results.

When stuff isn't working, you typically try harder. In fact, that's what some people tell you. They tell you work hard and work smart, as if that's a new idea you haven't thought of before.

The fact of the matter is this: many church leaders are tired because they are doing too much. They are leading multiple programs and ministries, all to varying degrees of effectiveness. The ministries they are most excited about don't get enough attention because the sideways things they are doing take their focus. The special events take the time from the regular (and most effective) ministries. It's a vicious cycle.

WHY DO YOU DO WHAT YOU DO?

When you look at your regular programs and ministries, can you answer the why questions? Why do you do them? Why are they a part of your ministry? Here are some common reasons why churches do the programs they do:

1. They have done them in the past.

Back in 1985, someone met Jesus at the Sunday night service, so let's keep doing it because it might happen again.

Three years ago, the food bank served 6,000 residents so we can't stop it now.

Sometimes pastors inherit ministries started by leaders in the past. I've talked to more than one pastor who felt forced to continue AWANAS, Vacation Bible School, The Wild Game Dinner, and the

Beth Moore Thursday morning studies. They are legacy ministries.

If they're effective then great. But "we've always done it this way" isn't good stewardship and holding on to a ministry just because it's been effective in the past is poor leadership.

2. Other people do them.

It's easy to look around your denomination and copy what other churches are doing. But just because a program or ministry is popular in your network doesn't mean it's the best thing for your church. Widen your gaze and consider other options.

3. You don't know of other alternatives.

It's pretty easy to get stuck in a rut when it comes to church programming. Maybe you're doing what you're doing because it's all you really know. If this is the case, start searching for something new.

We live in an incredible time. There are so many books, resources, and conferences. There are new networks and new relationships waiting for you. If you open your mind and you're willing to learn from new places, you might discover a far more effective type of program or ministry that could really work in your church.

4. You're afraid to do nothing.

A final reason churches do programs and ministries is because they're afraid to do nothing.

This was the case for me when we started our church in Atlanta.

Even though we were just one year into our church plant, we started a student ministry before we developed a leadership team and had a qualified leader. A student ministry is definitely not a bad thing, but we weren't ready.

Our entire Sunday morning experience was perfect for teenagers and we were in the midst of starting small groups. Parents of teenagers asked when we were starting a traditional student ministry like the other churches in town and I didn't have a good answer.

I gave in to the pressure and we started something.

At first, it worked. But after a few months, the lack of leadership and focus took its toll. We suffered for the next couple of years in this area. I was afraid of doing nothing, so we started a program. In the end, this transpired to be a big mistake.

It's okay to wait. And it's okay to say no for now. You don't have to do something just to do something, even if there's a big need.

Those are some of the common reasons why churches do programs and ministries. It's also the reason why churches end up with a menu of ministries that are all good but lack punch.

THE MISSING INGREDIENT

I'm convinced that one of the missing elements in most churches is evaluation.

We *do* so much, but we rarely stop to evaluate what we're doing in light of our mission and vision. We continue to fight and work and pray and lead, but we seldom pause to assess the situation and make adjustments.

But when it comes to evaluating church ministries, you don't line up the good programs on one side and put the bad ones on the other side. Because they are *all* good.

Unless your church has a devil worship ministry or a Tuesday Thievery small group, everything you're doing would line up on the good side. If you're assessing programs and ministries, there are probably very few things you would slide to the bad column. The measuring stick for your church has to be something more than good versus bad.

I'm not advocating that you cancel events and stop doing ministries so you can take it easy or so that your church can have an easier time. I am, however, advocating that you evaluate everything to see how effective it is when it comes to your mission and vision.

I would suggest systematically determining the merit, worth or significance of every program and ministry in your church.

Very little *real* evaluation happens in churches. Maybe it's because we don't want to hurt someone's feelings or maybe it's because we don't have the time. But rarely do we stop what we're doing for long enough to look at what we're doing.

But if you're willing to do this, you're going to step into leadership in a way that most churches never do.
Here's how to get started:

1. Make a list of every program, ministry, and regular event in your church.

When I was in high school, a teacher challenged me to make a list of 100 things I was thankful for. "This will be easy," I thought to myself as I started writing. The first 20 or 30 things did come pretty easily. *My parents. My health. My dog.*

But as the list got longer my task got harder. I scratched out the word "body" and added "fingers" and "toes." That's two for one. And then I realized I had ten fingers so I decided to list them individually. Even after this exercise in ridiculousness, I came to the conclusion that being thankful for everything is hard.

You need a list, and it might be harder than you think.

The first step in effective evaluating is to make a list of everything you're already doing. You can start on this right away. But one of the best ways to make sure your list is accurate is to include other people in the process. Ask your staff or pull together some key volunteers to work on this list.

At first, it might go like my thankfulness list. You'll start with listing the obvious programs and ministries then you'll make another little run. But just when you think you've got it all down, a whole new group of things will come to your mind. Your goal is to capture *everything*.

> » Printing your weekend handout...that's a regular program. Put it on the list.

> » Sending your weekly email newsletter...that's a regular event. Write it down.

» That Friday morning men's group. Even though they only use the facility and it's not an official church event, it's got to go on the list.

» Children's ministry, student ministry, women's ministry, church softball...everything you do must go on the list.

For some leaders, this exercise alone will provide incredible clarity. Very few church leaders ever see a list like this.

2. Answer questions about every item on the list.

Once you've listed every program, ministry, and event in your church, now the evaluation can begin. This will take a little more time, because you've got to ask these questions about everything on the list.

There are a lot of good evaluation questions, but here are two of my favorites:

KEY QUESTION #1: ARE THESE PROGRAMS EFFECTIVE IN HELPING US ACCOMPLISH OUR MISSION?

The key word in that question is "effective." As hard as it is, you *must* evaluate every ministry, program or activity in your church with objective eyes. You must set aside personal feelings and answer this tough question.

We're not talking about whether the programs are good or bad...

we're talking about whether they *work*. It's not helpful to know if people feel they are important, but it's very useful to know if they truly help the church accomplish its God-given mission.

Most people would hold up the church bulletin and say, "It looks good to me." But that's not the right evaluation question. You've got to ask, "How effective is this bulletin?" That's not a superficial question with a quick answer. You're going to have to dig deep. One of the pastors in my coaching network told me he recently went through this very experience. He realized people weren't really reading the printed bulletin so they stopped printing it. They saved more than $5,000 a year in printing costs and found more effective ways to distribute information.

Most pastors would listen to the music on Sunday and say, "It was great" or, "It wasn't good."

But those aren't the right questions. Evaluating quality is fine, but you've got to dig deeper in order to reach effectiveness. "How effective was our team at engaging people in worship?" is a far more important question to ask.

The second key word in this question is *mission*. When you're evaluating something, you've got to do it with your stated mission in mind. There are a lot of things that are positive, but if they don't help you accomplish your unique mission, they're sideways.

If accomplishments aren't tied to a larger mission, then they won't matter.

KEY QUESTION #2: *IF A NEW PASTOR OR LEADERSHIP TEAM TOOK OVER, WOULD THEY CONTINUE, STOP, OR CHANGE THIS?*

This is one of my favorite evaluation questions because it helps us disconnect and look at something objectively. This question comes from Andy Grove when he was the Chairman of the Board at Intel. He asked a fellow board member, "If we got kicked out and the board brought in a new CEO, what do you think he would do?" Grove knew their own involvement was tainting their decision-making. They needed to step outside of their own experience to make the wise choice.

The board's answer to this question led Intel to get out of the memory card business and focus on microchips. I'd say that was the right decision.

This is a great question for pastors and church leaders, who can easily become emotionally and spiritually attached to certain programs and ministries. By stepping back and thinking of your successor, you might be able to offer more objective evaluations and make better decisions.

Assign a letter grade.

Once you've made a list of all your regular activities and debated their merits in the light of vision and effectiveness, it's time to assign a letter grade.

Let me go ahead and warn you: this will feel weird. It's going to feel weird to put an "F" next to a ministry. You're going to feel that an awful rating is a failure. But the willingness to give real grades is the first step to making improvements.

For many of you, the most helpful thing you could do in your church would be to ruthlessly evaluate everything for the next three months. Don't try and start something new or start a new ministry. Instead, do a detailed inventory of all you're currently doing and make it more effective. Align your programs with the desired results. Make sure your ministries are helping you to accomplish the mission.

ACTION STEP

Visit churchfuel.com/streamline and download the Evaluation Pack. It's a series of six evaluation forms, including one to help you and your team evaluate your regular programs and ministries.

- 6 -

EVALUATE YOUR SPECIAL EVENTS

*We must assume that there is probably a better way
to do almost everything.*

— John Maxwell —

The point of this chapter is to give you some insanely practical tips for evaluating your special events. However, I want to start by talking you *out* of doing them.

So let's start with ice cream. That usually makes everything better.

There's an ice cream shop in Venezuela that sells more than 900 flavors of ice cream, including spaghetti and cheese. Now I like spaghetti, and I like ice cream, but the combination of the two sounds disgusting.

A gourmet French ice cream company sells caviar ice cream. I'm pretty sure that's a French rouse to get people to pay more money for ice cream. After all, it worked with Evian bottled water.

In Japan, you can treat yourself to *Taco Aisu*, which is basically octopus ice cream.

There are some strange ice cream flavors in the world, but do you know what the most *popular* flavor of ice cream is?

It's vanilla.

With all the interesting options out there, most people still opt for vanilla. It's hard to believe, but it's true. The simplest flavor of ice cream in the world is the most popular flavor of ice cream in the world.

It may be boring, but the simple stuff still works. It might even work the best.

The exotic, spectacular, and special events might get most of the press in the church world, but it's the weekend services, small groups, and children's ministry programs that have the most impact on people's lives. Those *regular* programs and *normal* activities have the greatest opportunity to impact your community.

Most people who visit your church are going to visit on a Sunday morning. That's one of your most ordinary regular events.

Most people who want to develop relationships will connect with a group or a class. Those regular ministries are kind of boring compared to the wild and crazy event ideas you read about online. But they're really effective.

Imagine taking all the time, energy, and resources you're investing into special events and pouring that into your regular programming. Imagine meetings focused on improving what happens every week instead of planning what's going to happen one time. Imagine a steady diet of weekly wins instead of busy season after busy season.

LESS IS MORE

When you talk to other pastors about what's happening in their church, they often tell you about special events. Maybe it's a children's event or a men's conference or an outreach event. Those kind of things are exciting, so we talk about them.

You hear about these events and you want to try them at your church. Maybe you put them on the calendar and start planning. Before you know it, you're recruiting people and spending money. People start working on the details. You start discussing it at length in your team meetings.

Before long, you're spending a good chunk of your time and energy on this special event. But it's sideways energy, because in the end the special event doesn't help you to accomplish your mission. People feel good because there is activity, but in the end there is little to show for it.

"Most churches do too much. In the absence of clear discipleship outcomes, we feel successful only with more attendance at more church stuff," writes Will Mancini. You may have a lot of church activities, but are those activities leading to clear discipleship outcomes? Is your activity producing action?

Take a look at the events in your church. Are they truly connected to the mission and vision or are they sideways? Events create sideways energy when:

» **There are no clear next steps for people to take.** If participation in the event is the win, you're probably creating a lot of movement without mission. Every event should have clear next steps for people.

» **Next steps don't lead into the life of the church.** Sometimes, there are next steps, but those next steps don't lead people into Gospel community or next steps at the church. Be careful.

» **It takes staff and leaders away from regular programs and ministries.** It's great if you can pull off an event for the community, but if your staff and leaders can't focus on regular programs and ministries, the overall church will suffer.

» **Attendance becomes the measuring stick.** I've heard so many churches communicate wins simply by talking about how many people showed up at the event. Gathering a crowd is a great starting point, but that's not enough.

» **The benefits of the event are available elsewhere.** We decided against doing a fall festival at our church for two reasons. First, there were several other churches doing them. And second, we didn't want to compete with trick or treating. In this case, there were tons of opportunities for people in our community. Duplicating an event would have been completely sideways. We could have attracted a crowd, but it wouldn't have helped us to accomplish our mission.

When I worked at The Rocket Company, we used a football analogy to communicate one of our core values. For a company based in the south and led by a raving Alabama fan, it's no wonder that football analogies made frequent appearances in our team meetings.

We talked about how trick plays were fun and made SportsCenter, but four-yard carries won the games. We wanted to run the ball every day, to string together a series of wins so we didn't have to rely on a trick play at the end of the game.

My fear is that a lot of churches are trying to sustain growth and health with trick plays. Maybe it's that special event that attracts a crowd and gives the appearance of life. Maybe it's the special offering that balances the budget, temporarily. Maybe it's the evangelist brought to town because there haven't been enough decisions lately. None of these things are bad, yet all of these things are bad if you're relying on them.

Too many events on your church calendar won't leave you with enough time to work on what truly matters. Every week, you have the opportunity to welcome guests, help people connect to God through worship, teach children about Jesus, facilitate Biblical community, and more. If you're too busy doing special stuff, you won't have time to do the regular stuff. And the regular stuff makes more of a long term impact.

In reality, a handful of special events can be a great thing. If you're running the ball consistently, maybe it's time for a play action pass. If special events are properly planned and they don't take people off focus, they can be a good thing for your church and community.

GREAT SPECIAL EVENTS

I've spent a great deal of time in this chapter trying to talk you out of doing too many special events and putting that energy into your regular programs. But not all events are sideways.

Not all events are off mission. So what kind of events are good for your church?

First, good events are effective events.

There's a huge difference between "good" and "effective." Most things that happen in a church are good, but very few things are effective.

Francis Chan says, "Our greatest fear should not be of failure but of succeeding at things in life that don't really matter." That's a powerful principle, and it should encourage us to live lives that honor God.

But that same principle applies to church leaders, too. A successful event should be much more than well-attended or well-executed. It should be effective. In other words, it should work.

When you talk about the effectiveness of events, you've got to do it in the context of your mission and vision. If the vision of your church is to get people connected in Biblical community, how effective is your event at that purpose? If the vision of your church is to launch campuses in nearby towns, how effective is your special event at moving towards that goal?

Move past attendance and get past quality to look under the hood of your special events. How effective are they at evangelism, discipleship, or missions? How well do they actually work? Don't ask if they are "good," dig deep and measure effectiveness.

A night of worship, or a small group kickoff, or a week-long children's camp might help you to accomplish the mission of your church. If these types of events contribute to your vision, they might be good.

Second, healthy events are evaluated events.

When a big event is over, there's a feeling of relief for everyone involved. All the prayer, planning, and the hard work is over. It's time to rest or move on to the next thing.

But when the event is done, you're not done. It's time to evaluate.

The failure to evaluate is one of the biggest reasons ineffective events become a part of the life of the church. "We've always done this," becomes the rally cry.

To keep this part of the process from feeling like a tacked-on, extra step at the end, make it a part of the planning process from the beginning. When you're creating your event timeline, go ahead and schedule your post-event surveys and evaluation meetings. Make feedback and evaluation a part of the event right from the start. And if you're not willing to do honest evaluation after the event, don't schedule it in the first place.

QUESTIONS TO HELP YOU EVALUATE SPECIAL EVENTS AND PROGRAMS

We've already said that quality and attendance aren't good enough measuring sticks. Those are good things, but you've got to dig much deeper and ask more poignant questions.

When the event is over, pull some people together and conduct a thorough and honest evaluation. If you're a visionary leader, you might rush past this important step as you move on to the next thing. But evaluation is absolutely critical.

You need to hear from participants and volunteers. You need to give your leaders the opportunity to share their experiences.

Here are some questions to guide your discussion:

» How does this event help us accomplish our mission?

» How does this event help us reach our goal?

» Is there a clear objective and defined win?

» Is this a quality event?

» What does this event truly cost?

» Is there a better option?

» If we weren't already doing this event, would we do it?

» How do we measure success?

» How effective was our internal communication?

» How effective was our external communication and promotion?

» Did people take a next step after the event?

» What letter grade would we give each part of the event?

» What are the long-term benefits?

» What do the volunteers say can be approved?

» What do the attenders say can be approved?

You've heard people say, "Practice makes perfect." And you've heard people respond, "Only carefully evaluated practice makes perfect." When it comes to events, the more you do them the more necessary it is to evaluate them for effectiveness.

Say no to events. Say yes to effective, carefully evaluated events with clear next steps for people that help a church accomplish its mission and vision.

ACTION STEP

The action step here is the same as the last chapter. That's good news for those of you who skipped it. Visit churchfuel.com/forms and download Evaluation Forms. It's a series of six evaluation forms, including one to help you and your team evaluate special events. Use this form to evaluate your next big event.

- 7 -

INVOLVE OUTSIDERS

Give me six hours to chop down a tree and I will spend the first four sharpening the axe.

- Abraham Lincoln -

One year into our church plant, I joined a coaching network made up of a group of pastors. We met once a month and talked about church leadership. During this coaching network, the leader said, "If you want people to be on the same page then create an actual page."

That sentence stuck with me and directly led to the creation of Docs and Forms, a resource that has helped over two thousand church leaders. Of course, I learned a lot through this network, but this one sentence made a huge difference.

A few years later, our church was stuck and needed a plan to grow. We hired a consultant to come in and work with us for a full day to create some new systems and structures for leadership and discipleship. We had some smart people on our team, but I still wanted the advice of an outsider who could see the things we missed. An outside facilitator with fresh ideas helped us accomplish far more than we could have accomplished on our own.

In 2011, my business partner and I went to a coaching group in Phoenix to spend time with other leaders. The mastermind group was pretty expensive, but the results were amazing. We learned many things, including a meeting system that helped our company grow from $450,000 to over $2 million in annual revenue. Coaching was directly tied to success.

When I look back on the key growth moments in life, ministry and business, advice from outsiders played a pivotal role.

FIVE REASONS YOU NEED TO INVOLVE OUTSIDERS

You're a smart person and a good leader. I know that because you're reading this book. Bad leaders don't pick up books on strategies and systems. Bad leaders don't want to get better. Smile, because you're one of the good guys!

You've already taken a huge step to get better as a leader and see healthy growth in your church. But if you want to reach your full potential, you're going to need the hands-on involvement of outsiders.

Here are three reasons you should involve outsiders.

1. Fresh Thinking and New Ideas

When you're *in* the organization, you sometimes miss what's right in front of you. It's not because you're uninformed, it's just because you're in it.

Ed Catmull is the President of Pixar and the author of a fantastic leadership book called *Creativity, Inc.* In this book, Catmull describes the Pixar Braintrust—a group of people who provided feedback and ideas on movies to the director.

At various points in a movie's development, the director shows the project to the Braintrust. Then, he listens. The Braintrust doesn't have the authority to make changes, but they provide the director with fresh perspective and ideas.

Catmull says the Braintrust is one of the key factors of Pixar's success. They have created a culture that encourages fresh thinking. By involving other artists and directors, particularly those not involved in a project on a day-to-day basis, they dramatically improve their movies.

If you want fresh thinking and new ideas, you're going to need to give people time. Pixar can't rush a movie to box office success—they have to plan, work, meet, review, and hundreds of other steps. In your church, the more you can plan ahead, the more you can involve outsiders and expose yourself to new ways of thinking. If you want helpful feedback, you've got to give people time to share it.

2. Validation and Encouragement

When I work with churches, I sometimes tell them things they already know but need to hear from an outsider. This isn't a waste of time or money. It's a small price to pay for peace and confidence.

At first, I used to take it personally when people told me they didn't learn anything new from me. Then I realized they didn't need new information, they needed encouragement and the confidence to lead.

It's amazing how an outsider can provide confirmation. Maybe you have a gut feeling about something. Sharing that idea with a group of leaders and hearing their encouragement can give you the permission to act.

3. Solutions to Existing Problems

I participated in a monthly coaching group in Atlanta made up of some other Christian leaders. Part of our day was spent helping each other with our unique problems.

At a recent meeting, I shared what was happening in my life and the group provided tons of wise counsel and helped me make the right decision. It was a big decision and I was confused. This group of people, who all paid to be in the same room with each other, provided amazing insight and helped me to navigate the problem.

When you involve outsiders, you invite their unique experiences and perspectives into your problem. You expose yourself to new ideas and thoughts. Simply put, you get better.

WHERE TO INVOLVE OUTSIDERS

When you learn to value the opinions of those who aren't involved in the day-to-day operation of the church, you'll find all sorts of environments where their insight can really help. Here are a few:

1. You Can Involve Outsiders in Sermon Planning

Every church has a fact-checker—that one theologically educated individual who seems intent on correcting every missed reference or fact in the sermon. Typically, these individuals mention something as they head to their car or send an email that will be waiting for you on Monday morning. Their sense of timing is impeccable, firing off corrections at the most inopportune times.

For the longest time, I avoided these people and openly chided them to get involved in a real way that made a real difference. Instead of serving in the nursery, they seemed intent on being a human Snopes for sermons.

It's possible these people are crazy. But what's far more likely is that God has given them a great mind and a passion for the accurate interpretation of Scripture. Rather than marginalize their contributions and turn into a passive/aggressive critic, I needed to find a place for them to serve according to their unique gift mix.

Most churches are great at finding places for people to serve with their hands. We need to get better at finding places for people to serve with their minds.

So, I created a brand new volunteer opportunity for the seminary-type, Bible-study-loving, intellectual thinkers in our church. I brought them right into the sermon planning process.

As we started work on a new series, I invited a group of people (including outsiders) to come to a structured meeting to talk about messages. I asked them to bring books, commentaries, and articles relating to the series we were starting. My job at this meeting was simple—to sit and listen. Instead of criticisms and critiques, these people began bringing helpful and useful information. A lot of it actually made its way into sermons. This meeting only happened a few times, but the presence of outsiders made it better.

You could invite another pastor, an unchurched person in your community, or a teenager to meetings like this. You'll find their insight amazing.

2. You Can Involve Outsiders in Strategy Sessions

There are times in the life of every church when a professional, outside opinion is what's needed to breakthrough a barrier and reach the next level. Professional athletes at the top of their game need coaches in order to win, and so do churches.

Professional consultants who know what they're doing can help you get organized around your mission. Yes, this costs money, but the value you receive far outweighs the cost. For example, if you were ill you could ask your friend for medical advice, or you could visit a doctor who has been to medical school and knows what he's talking about. You can "pick the brain" of someone who's not prepared and who doesn't give your issue their best brainpower or you can hire an expert to work on your behalf.

I know you've heard the phrase "you get what you pay for." This is definitely true in church leadership. If you want to truly grow as a leader, create healthy systems in your church, or lead your church through a large opportunity, engage the professional services of someone who can help.

Here's when you should bring in a professional:

» When you're making a major, church-altering decision

» When you're launching another campus

» When you're looking to raise a significant sum of money

» When you need to facilitate a major change

» When you need to restructure the staff

» When you want to make significant improvements

» When you need to create healthy systems.

3. You Can Involve Outsiders in Service Evaluation

When you're in the middle of it, it's easy to miss things. It's natural, because you're used to seeing what you normally see. It's normal, but that doesn't mean it's effective.

You're used to the way you do things, but that comfort level might be blinding you to what everybody else sees. Your impression of how things are working might not match the first impression of that first time guest you're trying to reach.

That's why you should bring in a secret shopper who will see things that you miss. When you bring in a secret shopper, they can give you fresh perspective on:

» First impressions

» Pre-service experience

- » Signage

- » Hospitality

- » Facility

- » Kids check in

- » Children's ministry environments

- » Music

- » Sermon

- » Branding

- » Follow up process.

Bringing someone in to say "that was good" or "that needs work" isn't helpful. When I evaluate a service, I spend a great deal of time making specific recommendations, even pointing people to specific solutions or products that can improve their overall experience.

Outside opinions can help you take a giant leap forward in the quality of your service and the effectiveness of your ministry.

ACTION STEP

You can download a series of evaluation forms from churchfuel.com/ streamline. There are forms to help you evaluate your sermon, special event or church service. Give these forms to others and ask for feedback.

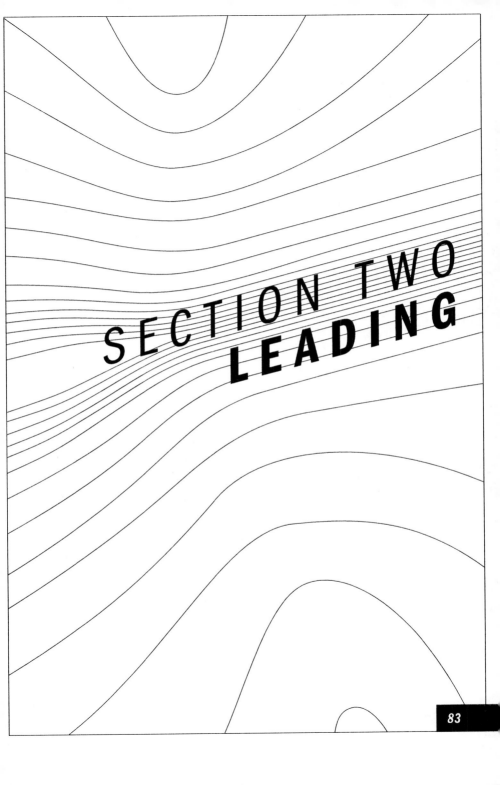

SECTION TWO
LEADING

- 8 -

BUILD YOUR ORG CHART

The achievements of an organization are the results of the combined effort of each individual.

- Vince Lombardi -

What exactly are systems and how do they work in a church? Let me give you a few metaphors.

» Systems are like pipes inside the wall of a house. You don't want to see pipes, but without them, the toilet won't flush. Pipes may not be pretty, but they're incredibly useful.

» The body is a collection of several systems. There's the digestive system, reproductive system, and neurological system. All of these systems work together. When one gets out of whack, the whole body suffers.

» We live on Earth, which is the third planet from the sun in the solar system, created by God with a specific set of parameters. A slight variation in the Earth's axis and we spiral into space.

» My computer runs on an operating system (OS 10.9.5 to be exact). If I have a problem with my operating system, my software won't work. Downloads and apps are useful, but without an operating system, they're useless.

Some people love systems and processes. Others would rather spend an hour in a dentist's chair with reruns of Golden Girls playing on the television. But whether you like them or loathe them, you need them.

Systems don't come naturally to me. I've learned to see the value, mostly because I've suffered from the lack of them in ministry. I was a disorganized youth pastor that got by on passion and communication skills. I was a visionary church planter, who learned the hard way that you couldn't simply will your way out of problems.

As a pastor of a growing church, I realized I couldn't preach my way out of a systems problem. A greater vision couldn't solve our systems problems either. If we were going to get traction, it was going to take systems, processes, and a little bit of intentional organization.

If you're not naturally organized, there's hope for you because church growth (and health) isn't tied to your personality. You might be an introvert, but that doesn't mean your church can't be friendly. You might not like singing, but that doesn't mean your church can't embrace worship. And you might not be naturally organized, but that doesn't mean you can't align and organize your church for greater effectiveness.

The mission of the local church is eternally important. That's why it's worth stepping out of your personality to work on the ministry.

That's why it's worth bringing clarity, focus, and a little structure to your staff.

An org chart is one of the first systems you should work on. When you put your structure on paper, it will allow you to work on it without getting involved in the emotional struggle of leading people.

Some people push back on the idea of an org chart, believing it to be limiting, a waste of time, or too static to capture the ethos of real church leadership. And while there are definitely some valid concerns with over-systemizing something that's inherently relational, most of the push back against organizational structure comes from a misunderstanding of the intent.

I want to talk about what an org chart is and some best practices for creating one for your church. But let's start with discussing what an org chart is *not*. Your org chart is not:

A communication policy. In the military, there's a chain of command. It's not appropriate for a Private to go straight to a General with an issue. I know about this because I've seen the movie, A Few Good Men. In many corporate cultures, there's a similar chain of command, with levels and layers between groups of employees. A sales associate can't talk to the CEO.

But a clear org chart in your church doesn't need to hinder communication among the team. In fact, healthy church teams have open door policies and cultivate an environment where anyone can talk to anyone.

A never-changing document. While an org chart can describe reality and provide clarity, it's not a static document on par with the church constitution and bylaws. A good org chart is a "right now" document, so don't write your org chart in stone.

A diagram of importance. It looks like common sense to assume the person at the top of the org chart is the most important, and the positions at the bottom are there to support the others.

But a staff structure isn't like the royalty hierarchy in the United Kingdom. All positions and roles in a church are important. In *1 Corinthians 12*, Paul describes the church as the body of Christ. Each member of the body is important. Likewise, everybody on the staff at a church should be treated with the same honor and respect. The org chart is there to clarify roles, responsibilities, and relationships, not importance.

Now that we've talked about what an org chart is *not*, let's look into what it *is* and why you should create one.

An org chart is a simple, graphical representation of your staff structure. It's a picture, which is often easier to understand and communicate than a list of policies, which describe who is leading the church.

Here's what a clear org chart will do for you:

A clear org chart provides clarity. While the church is a spiritual enterprise, it's also a company. It's *more than* a company, but it's *at least* a company. Good companies have clear roles, and those roles are defined on a clear org chart. It's important for leaders and managers to provide clarity for everyone on their team, and an org chart starts the process.

We're going to talk more about clarity in Chapter 10.

A clear org chart helps you know who to hire. As you build an org chart, it's likely that you'll notice holes. These are opportunities to bring new people onto the team. Great org charts identify the next hires and show how they'll fit on the team.

In fact, creating a clear org chart should be a part of your hiring process. You should never hire someone without knowing where they fit.

A developed org chart is a prayer list. As a leader, you should be on the lookout for people to fill needs that fit your mission and vision, and you should constantly pray for God to send the right people.

In addition, the people who are on your org chart are like sheep in your flock. Pray for them before trying to lead them. Pastor them before trying to manage them. A line connecting two boxes on an org chart doesn't just represent leadership, but also documents the flow of pastoral care.

Provide a snapshot view of your church leadership. It's easier to see what's missing, and it's especially useful in growing churches or churches that want to grow. Churches that struggle to structure for growth often have a muddy org chart, or no org chart at all.

HOW TO CREATE A GOOD ORG CHART

If you have one, it's time to pull it out and refresh it. If you don't have one, it's time to build your beta version. As you get to work, here are some things to consider:

1. **Start by sketching your current reality.** Whether it's documented on paper or not, you have a current

organizational structure. Start by drawing that out in a flow chart. Write what's currently unwritten and begin to structure what's currently free form.

2. **Write down positions, not people.** Create boxes for positions, not necessarily people you have. If you have one person fulfilling two roles on your org chart, go ahead and draw two boxes. Thinking positions instead of people will keep some of the emotion out of it.

3. **Wrestle with balance.** As you build your org chart, it will be easy to see if certain areas are over-represented with staff and leaders, and if others need some leadership. If the majority of your people are focused on leading the church service, you might need to address leadership in family ministry.

4. **Your org chart can include full time pastors, part time staff, and key volunteers.** Everyone that occupies a place of leadership should show up on your org chart.

5. **Use diagramming software.** I use diagram software such as Omnigraffle to make charts and flowcharts, but there are a lot of free web options for creating charts and diagrams. Go ahead and get used to a tool, because you can use it to create other systems and strategies in your church as well.

Here is a sample org chart I created for a fictitious church. I used the color yellow to designate roles on the leadership team. You could also use colors to designate part time employees or key volunteers.

Cross City Church Org Chart

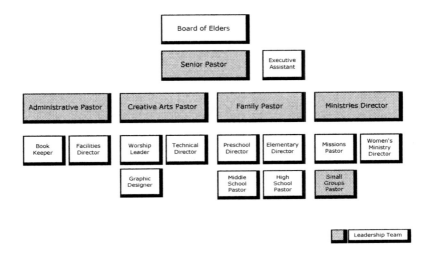

Figure 3: Sample Org Chart. You can download this template at churchfuel.com/streamline.

Do you need to create an org chart to reflect the leadership structure of your church? Or is your current org chart out of date and in dire need of updating? If you answered yes to either of these questions, dive in. You'll find the process of creating or updating opens the door to helpful conversations and healthy changes.

ACTION STEP

*Take out a sheet of paper or head to a dry erase board
and build the beta version of your org chart. Use it to think, plan,
and dream about who God wants to be in leadership at your church.*

- 9 -

WRITE AN EMPLOYEE HANDBOOK

In the successful organization,
no detail is too small to escape close attention.

- Lou Holtz -

Remember what you thought that one time someone suggested that all you had to do was work one hour on Sunday? You didn't want to turn the other cheek; you wanted to throw the other fist.

Pastors don't work one hour a week. You don't even have one job title.

You're a counselor, administrator, preacher, leader, and manager. Sometimes you're a janitor or accountant. You might also be the small group's pastor or the youth pastor or the fill in worship leader. The job title of PASTOR is broad.

Because being a pastor involves all sorts of things, your daily schedule is often all over the place. In the morning you're prepping for a sermon and in the afternoon you're refereeing a fight between two church members. Somewhere in between you try and read church leadership books on getting traction.

Let me see if I can provide some clarity around your job title.

I believe the Senior Pastor is the Chief Clarity Officer of the church. They may not have taught you that in seminary, but years of ministry without focus and unmet potential is the alternative. You have to provide clarity to your church and to your team, because it won't occur naturally. This is one of the most under-appreciated, under-valued parts of a Pastor's job But if you embrace it, your church will gain a crazy amount of traction.

Your staff needs to know what, out of all their responsibilities and tasks, is the most important. They need clear expectations and focused goals. And they need you to lead.Creating clarity for your staff can take a light year leap forward with an Employee Handbook.

In corporations and businesses, the Employee Handbook is a legal document filled with fluff and boring information on company policies and procedures. It's rarely read and much less used. Maybe they teach boring writing in law school.

When I set out to create an Employee Handbook for the Rocket Company, I decided to keep it fun. Of course, it had to be informative and we needed to talk about policies, procedures, and paychecks, but I wanted this to be a conversational document that would be read and enjoyed. Here's what I wrote in the introduction:

> *This document is designed to provide you with*
> *general information about working here...and to do*

*so in a way that won't make you wish you were at
the dentist for your first cleaning in five years.*

*The goal of this document is to create clarity.
It's not a formal contract - it's a list of two-way
expectations. Because we want to be on the same
page, we decided to put the words on an actual
page.*

*I must say that one document, no matter how well-
written, can cover every little thing about working
here. It's impossible to cover every subject.*

*So if you need to know something that isn't covered
here, just ask.*

*For what it's worth, we reserve the right to change
or interpret these policies as needed. But we will
let you know if something changes.*

Are you ready? Let's blast off.

The rest of the handbook continued in a helpful but slightly humorous tone.

You might not be a writer, but you need to write an Employee Handbook. It should be given to and discussed with everyone on your team, and you should use it in your hiring process.

Here are some things that should go in your Employee Handbook:

» **Your Mission and Vision:** Since this is a foundational document for your team, your Employee Handbook should start by describing your mission and vision. We're going to talk about the difference between those two things in Chapter 23

» **Core Values:** Next, talk about the core values of your church and what it looks like to reflect those core values in the work place.

» **Causes for Termination:** Can an employee be fired for smoking cigarettes or playing blackjack? What's the rule on drinking alcohol? Are you allowed to discuss salaries and benefits with other team members? Are staff members expected to tithe? While you can't cover every situation, you can work hard to clarify expectations. Do this on the front end and you'll prevent a ton of heartache on the backend. If your state is an at-will state (you'll need to check on this), you could include language like this:

Nobody is forcing you to work here. That's why we maintain an employment-at-will policy. Just as you're free to end your job and move on to greener pastures, we reserve the right to end an employment relationship with any employee at any time for any reason.

» **Resignation Process:** When you're hiring a new employee, it's weird to think about letting them go or watching them leave. But it happens a lot. A great Employee Handbook will pre-determine this process. This is where you can ask for two-weeks notice or clarify the expectations around the departure.

» **Getting Paid:** This is often the most interesting part of the Employee Handbook for employees because it's where you describe how paychecks work. Clarify your pay period and direct deposit procedures.

» **Description of Benefits:** In addition to describing paycheck procedures, your handbook should describe available benefits and when they kick in. Here's how we described the benefits available to employees.

Full-time employees are also eligible for:

The 401(k) Plan. If you work at least 1,000 hours a year, you can participate in our 401(k) plan. We'll match your contributions, up to 3% of your total compensation. You're fully vested on your start date, which means you can start saving for that RV trip across the country right away.

Health Insurance. We will pay 100% of your premium for Medical and Dental Health Insurance. You can purchase additional coverage for your and your family or add vision coverage for you and your family through an automatic payroll deduction. Medical coverage is provided by _____, and Dental and Vision Insurance are provided by _____. Summaries describing the Medical, Dental, and Vision plans are available upon request. Hope you like to read, because medical documents are not nearly as fun to read as this handbook

Short-Term Disability Insurance. We will pay 100% of the premium for short-term disability insurance. Maternity related absences are covered under this short-term disability plan. If approved, 60% of your weekly earnings may be continued for up to 12 weeks, at a maximum of $1,000 per week. The benefit is tax-free. A summary describing the details of the plan are available upon request.

Long Term Disability Insurance. We will pay 100% of the premium for long term disability insurance, providing salary continuation in the event of an approved illness or injury lasting more than 90 consecutive days. If approved for long term disability pay, 60% of your monthly earnings may be continued up to age 65, at a maximum of $10,000 per month. The benefit is tax-free. A summary describing the details of the plan are available upon request.

» **Time off Policy:** Be clear about how much paid time off people will receive. You can also clarify what days the office is closed. We opted for a simple time off policy, but the important thing is that you clarify it. Here's what we said:

We encourage every employee to take vacation. Rest is Biblical - it's actually one of the Ten Commandments, and those are pretty important. Each full-time employee gets fifteen paid personal days to use however you like. Take a family trip. Watch TV. Clean your house or plant a garden. Whatever you do to relax is good for you and good with us. Each part-time employee gets seven paid personal days to use however you like.

» **Can't Miss Dates:** Make sure everyone knows what Sundays can't be missed. Don't wait around until Easter weekend and be frustrated that your children's director wants to go and visit their family. Communicate the Easter Weekend expectations in advance. Write down the dates of your annual staff retreat and quarterly planning retreats so people know in advance and can make plans. Put on the Chief Clarity Officer hat and clarify expectations for these retreats.

» **Office Hours:** Do people need to be in the office for 40-hours a week? Can they work from home? Your Employee Handbook is the place to clarify this, and conversations in advance will prevent much more awkward conversations later.

» **Confidentiality:** When people work in a church, they have access to the personal information of a lot of people. They will also be privy to private conversations and records. So it's important to clarify your policy on this. I recommend that every church asks employees to sign a confidentiality agreement.

Those are a few of the things that should go in your Employee Handbook. Update it every year and make sure everyone on your staff is on the same page. If you do this correctly, your Employee Handbook can be a fresh document that describes what it's like to work at your church.

ACTION STEP

You can download a sample employee handbook at churchfuel.com/streamline. Remember, this is a sample for inspirational purposes, but there's a lot there you could use. Use it as a template or a guide.

- 10 -

CREATE A HIRING PROCESS

*"The most important decisions that business people make are not **what** decisions, but **who** decisions."*

- Jim Collins -

There are few things that help an organization grow, such as hiring the right person to do the right job. It's amazing when you identify a need and God raises up a person to meet that need. The church becomes stronger because someone is empowered to use their gifts.

When you have the right people working in the right roles doing the right tasks, there's amazing synergy. Staff meetings are fun and ministry is more meaningful because you're doing it with people you love. For a long time, I focused on "what" and neglected the "who." I failed to realize it was people, not processes that would lead to traction. After all, processes without people to run them, are useless.

The right people will make ministry more fun for you. And it will help your church be more effective, too. A clear and focused staff will help your church reach people for Christ and help them grow in faith.

But there are few things that will sidetrack your church in the same way as a bad hire.

Too many times, we bring in someone to do a job only to realize—in the end—that it wasn't a good fit. It seems like I talk to at least one pastor each week who's really wrestling through a staff situation.

Sometimes, it's a new hire that's not working out. Sometimes, there needs to be some reshuffling or reorganization. And sometimes, there's someone on the team that needs to go. Most pastors I know would rather work on a message, participate in a team meeting, or do some real ministry than deal with staffing issues. Staff issues have a way of draining the life out of leaders.

That's why you need to create a hiring process.

I'm not talking about getting your next hire right. That's silver bullet thinking. I'm talking about creating a strong, healthy process for bringing people onto the team.

The hiring process you create is far more important than the next hire you make because a hiring process will guide you every time, not just the *next* time. And, of course, a better hiring process will go a long way to ensuring you get your next hire right.

THREE BENEFITS OF A GOOD HIRING PROCESS

1. **It takes the emotion out of hiring people.** Hiring someone is an emotional process. On the surface, someone can appear to possess all of the skills and be a great fit on the team. They can have the character, competence, and chemistry you're looking for. But the chances are, you're blinded by a great need. The more pain you feel from an unfilled need, the more tempted you'll be to fill it with someone that's not exactly right for the role. Even though you know it's better to have nobody than the wrong person, it doesn't feel like that in the middle of it.

2. **You can use it over and over again.** Like most systems, once you create it and implement it, you can use it time and time again. You're not just solving one problem, you're solving a recurring problem. In fact, your hiring process will get better every time you use it.

3. **You make better hiring decisions.** The better your process, the better hires you'll make. And the greater likelihood that the role will be filled by the right person who really adds to the team.

I strongly recommend you to create a hiring process that fits your culture. But to get you thinking in that direction, I want to share a process I created for our team. You can start with this process and tweak it to fit your church.

STEP ONE:
IDENTIFY A POSITION OF NEED

This seems like an obvious step, but there's more here than you might realize. You see, it's easy to *feel* like you need to hire someone. But, bringing a new person on the team needs to accomplish much more than meeting a feeling of need. You must think through exactly what this person will do, who they will work for and work with, and how this new role will affect the team dynamics.

Before you begin the process of filling a role, you need to think long and hard about the specifics of the job and how that role fits. Ask and answer specific questions, such as:

» What will this person actually do?

» How is this task being accomplished now?

» Who will they work for? Who will they work with?

» How will this new hire affect the team dynamic?

Never hire someone without a clear org chart. A new employee needs to understand how they fit into the leadership structure of the church. A lack of clarity will create muddy waters and a lack of effectiveness.

So before you start asking around or posting on websites, make sure you have a clear org chart. We talked about that in Chapter 8.

STEP TWO:
CREATE A DETAILED JOB PROFILE

This is one of the most important steps in the process. Too many times, we hire "good" people who are friends, but they lack focus. Without that clarity, hard workers will spend their time doing things that aren't that important. And leaders will get frustrated without a clear definition of a win.

So your job is to create a clear job profile that answers key questions. This might be more detailed than you're used to, but in this step two things are happening. Firstly, you're forcing yourself to think through the role and goal of this position. Secondly, you're setting up a new hire for a win. This job profile should cover things like:

» The mission and vision of the church (be specific). Lots of people should agree with your mission, but not everyone should buy into your vision.

» The role of the position and how it relates to the rest of the team.

» Goals and expectations. Communicate your expectations for this position in advance, before you start talking to anyone.

» Key Performance Indicators. This is common in the business world, but for some reason, we get all touchy feely with ministry positions. However, the bottom line is there are performance expectations for this role, so clarify them in advance.

» Candidate profile. Describe the ideal candidate. Try to weed people out from even applying with your language.

» Job details. Describe the office environment, work hours, and so on.

I know this seems like a lot of information, but if you do this hard work at the beginning, you will save yourself a lot of heartache in the end.

STEP THREE:
SEARCH FOR CANDIDATES

Now that you know how the position fits on your team and you've done the hard work of creating a job profile, it's time to begin searching for candidates.

Before I continue, you might want to engage the help of a professional. A search firm or consultant sounds expensive, but in 99% of the cases it's far less expensive than making the wrong hire.

But if you're setting out to do this on your own, you'll want to create a search system. Here's what I recommend:

1. Put up a blog post or a landing page describing the job. Provide as much information as possible up front.

2. Embed a form on the page so people can send their information. Wufoo is a good tool and you could also use Google Forms.

3. Ask pre-screening questions on your form. If you like their answers, you'll move to a formal interview process. This is just a pre-screening form. I shared some ideas below.

4. Email the page to every pastor you know. Post it on social media. Post it on job boards. Share the link with your church (they may know people). Get as many eyeballs as possible to this page.

PRE SCREENING QUESTIONS

1. What forms of social media do you use?
2. What compelled you to apply for a position?

3. How does our company mission fit with your personal calling?
4. What is your story?
5. What are you currently learning? From whom?
6. What are your strengths and weaknesses?
7. What books have you read in the past 12 months?
8. What do you like to do for fun?
9. Where do you currently work and what do you do?
10. What have you learned in your current position?
11. What were your major accomplishments in this role?
12. What do you love about your job? What do you not love about it?
13. What are you looking for in your next job?
14. What are your results from _The Predictable Success Quiz?_

When people fill out the form, make sure you take them to a confirmation page or send them a confirmation email. You need to be clear about how you will follow up. Will everyone receive a personal response or will you contact them if interested. Either way is okay...just be clear.

STEP FOUR:
INTERVIEW

Once you've publicized the job and have a list of potential candidates, it's time to start the interview process. But one interview isn't enough. You should actually do five interviews.

Whoa. I know that sounds crazy, but it's not as overwhelming as it seems.

Every candidate for every position goes through the same process,

completes each interview, and answers the same questions. You
don't come up with new questions or a new process for each
candidate or for each job. You do this same process every time. As
you can imagine, the process itself and your decision making will
get better and better every time you go through it.

Interview #1: Screening

The purpose of this interview is to determine if you want to
seriously consider this person for the role. The goal here is to
eliminate people as quickly as possible. Ask the same four questions
to each candidate. Stay on track and keep pushing for specific
examples. Ask, "How" and say, "Tell me more." You can do this in
person or over Skype video. It's okay to use the phone, but if you
can look at the person, it's better. Here are the questions to ask
during this interview:

» What are your career goals?

» What are you really good at professionally? (push for 8-12
positives with examples. Press for time when they are
indecisive)

» What are you not good at or not interested in doing
professionally?

» Who were your last five bosses, and how will they each rate
your performance on a 1-10 scale when I talk to them?

Stay on these questions, but dive into them. If someone says, "I just
want to help people" to the career goal question, keep pushing as
that's not a good enough answer. If they give shallow or expected

answers, keep digging because you're looking for specifics.

Interview #2: Patterns

Past behavior is the best predictor of future performance. If you want to know how someone will perform in a role, look at how they performed in the last role. Sure, things may be different and your culture might not be the same as their last church culture, but by in large people approach work the same way. So in this interview, you're looking for patterns of behavior to make predictions about how someone is likely to perform in the future.

This is the main interview phase, and you really only need to ask four questions. Sure, you can talk about favorite movies or books or try to come up with questions that will assess cultural fit. But most of those questions are silly, and you'll be able to assess cultural fit by hanging out in social situations. Can all those canned interview questions and just ask these five questions:

» What were you hired to do?

» What accomplishments are you most proud of? Exceptional people tend to talk about outcomes connected to expectations. Mediocre people tend to talk about events, people or job aspects not related to results.

» What were some low points during that job?

» Who were the people you worked with? Further questions to press here include, what was it like to work with your boss? What will they say is your biggest strength or weakness? How would you rate the team you inherited? What changes did you make? Did you hire or fire anyone?

How would you rate the team when you left?

» Why did you leave that job?

Go though this series of questions for every chapter or story in their life. Walk through career history chronologically. This should take two to three hours. You don't need to ask a bunch of questions, but you do need to ask these questions over and over again.

Interview #3: Results

This interview is focused on the desired outcome of the position. Your mission is to talk about expectations of the job and drill down on how the candidate has performed in related areas in the past. You're not just looking to see what they *think* they will do, but what they have done in similar environments with similar objectives.

» The purpose of this interview is to talk about _____ (name a specific outcome or competency)

» What are your biggest accomplishments in this area during your career?

» What are your insights into your biggest mistakes and lessons learned in this area?

While these interviews and questions should stay the same every time, you can involve different people in different phases. And if you're bringing in someone from out of town, you can do Interview #2 and Interview #3 in the same day. Just involve different people and change up the environment.

Hiring for a ministry position is much different than filling a corporate role, and it's likely you don't have a big Human Resources department. But you can learn a lot from the way great companies recruit, train, and lead their teams.

Interview #4: References

Once you have a strong candidate, it's time to talk to their previous boss or co-workers. This isn't a candidate interview, it's an interview of their references. I can't stress this enough...*always do this step.* Here are specific questions you should ask:

- » In what context did you work with the person?

- » What were the person's biggest strengths?

- » What were the person's biggest areas for improvement back then?

- » How would you rate his or her overall performance in that job on a 1-10 scale? What about his or her performance causes you to give that rating?

- » The person mentioned that he/she struggled with _____. Can you tell me more about that?

Interview #5: Relationships

This isn't an interview, but an opportunity to hang out in a non-interview setting to assess fit and culture. Other team members and spouses are involved, and this should happen outside a normal setting.

Remember, every person you hire adds to your team culture. Yes, your culture will heavily influence them but this goes both ways. There are few things that will disrupt a healthy leadership culture more than the wrong person at the table.

You don't have to be best friends with everyone that works at your church, but it shouldn't be awkward to hang out with them. Take them to dinner or dessert. Go to a baseball game. Hang out at a cookout. Find something relational and outside of the office and involve other people in a social setting.

Going through all of these steps can't guarantee you've made the right choice, but as you can imagine, it's far more likely that you'll make the right call after this process.

STEP FIVE:
JOB OFFER

Now that you've settled on the right person and they're interested in joining your team, it's time to make a formal job offer. Do this in writing and clarify all the details of employment. A simple letter will do the trick.

I can't stress this enough, but this hiring process should be used every time you hire a new person. You should certainly tweak it to fit your style and culture, but once it's ready, lock it in and leave it alone.

You will be tempted to skip steps to hire someone you know. You'll be tempted to move fast because a need is so apparent. But more times than not, you'll regret those decisions. A good system will help you make good decisions.

ACTION STEP

Visit churchfuel.com/streamline and download
this hiring process for free. Tweak and change it to fit your church.
You can use it every time you need to hire someone in your church.

- 11 -

CLARIFY ROLES FOR EVERYONE ON YOUR TEAM

In a balanced organization, working towards a common objective, there is success.

- Arthur Helps -

If you're a leader of people, you're in charge of providing continual clarity. You have to fight to protect the vision, and you have to fight to keep people focused on the parts of their job that mean the most when it comes to accomplishing that vision. The church, like any business, is prone to drift.

It's easy to drift from the mission.
It's easy to lose sight of the vision.
It's easy to wander from the things that matter most.

If this is true for a local church in general, it's definitely true for pastors and church leaders. Over time, clear jobs get muddied with extra responsibilities and tasks. Leaders lose sight of the things that really matter, dabbling in other programs and ministries that are slightly off base. Maybe it's a Spiritual ADD, but I think there's something in all pastors that lead us to chase every great opportunity.

For many pastors, clarity is muddy from the beginning, starting with the job description.

I love reading these documents, mostly because they're ridiculous. The other day I read a job description for a part time book-keeper, receptionist, and preschool director. All one part-time job! That seems like a pretty particular skill set. *We need you to be great with kids and a preschool educational background would be best, but we also need you to understand General Accounting Practices and you must have three years of experience with QuickBooks.*

Then, there are the qualifications. I'm not sure the Apostle Paul would be qualified to be the student pastor at a 50-person church based on some of the job postings I've seen. It reminds me of the old internet meme where an ancient Pastor Search Committee reports some of their findings. I'll shorten it so you don't have to read an entire internet meme.

> We've not been able to find a suitable candidate for this church, though we have one promising prospect still. We do appreciate all the suggestions from the church members, and we've followed up each one with interviews or by calling at least three references. The following is our confidential report on the present candidates:
>
> **Adam:** Good man but has problems with his wife. Also one reference told of how his wife and he enjoy walking nude in the woods.

Noah: Former pastorate of 120 years with no converts. Prone to unrealistic building projects.

Joseph: A big thinker, but a braggart, who believes in dream-interpreting, and has a prison record.

Moses: A modest and meek man, but poor communicator, even stuttering at times. Sometimes blows his stack and acts rashly. Some say he left an earlier church over a murder charge.

David: The most promising leader of all until we discovered the affair he had with his neighbor's wife.

Solomon: Great preacher but our parsonage would never hold all those wives.

Elijah: Prone to depression, and collapses under pressure.

Elisha: Reported to have lived with a single widow while at his former church.

Jeremiah: Emotionally unstable, alarmist, negative, always lamenting things, and reported to have taken a long trip to bury his underwear on the bank of a foreign river.

Jonah: Refused God's call into ministry until he was forced to obey by getting swallowed by a great fish. He told us the fish later spat him out on the shore near here. We hung up.

Peter: Too blue collar. Has a bad temper—even has been known to curse. Had a big run-in with Paul in Antioch. Aggressive, but a loose cannon.

Paul: Powerful CEO type leader and fascinating preacher. However, short on tact, unforgiving with younger ministers, harsh, and has been known to preach all night.

Timothy: Too young.

Jesus: Has had popular times, but once when his church grew to 5000 he managed to offend them all and this church dwindled down to twelve people. Seldom stays in one place very long. And, of course, he's single.

Judas: His references are solid. A steady plodder. Conservative. Good connections. Knows how to handle money. We're inviting him to preach this Sunday. Possibilities here.

That's a silly example of how ridiculous church job descriptions can be. Have you read the long bullet lists of duties on some job descriptions? They read more like wish lists rather than realistic responsibilities. Here's a list of duties for an associate pastor at a church of about 200 members. I saw this on a pastoral search website:

» Lead, support and oversee spiritual formation and spiritual growth in the church.

» Lead, support and oversee the connections ministry in the church, ensuring people who visit are connected to a group, serving team and give generously to all ministries of the church.

» Lead the prayer ministry.

» Develop a new ministry to singles and young adults, with worship and teaching.

» Oversee the women's ministry, including weekly Bible

studies and special events, helping recruit volunteers as needed.

» Be on call one day a week for hospital and pastoral care visits.

» Meet regularly with the senior pastor and other leaders as necessary.

» Participate regularly in Sunday morning and Sunday night worship services.

And just to cover all bases and punctuate the absurdity, the last bullet point is often something like "other duties as described by your supervisor." It's there as if to say, "We've tried to list every random thing that might be useful to the church, but just in case we missed something, we want you to know there's a lot of other random things you will probably do."

I'm all for encouraging a "get it done no matter what" mentality among your team, but you can't ask everyone to do everything and expect anything to be done with excellence.

We bring people onto the team and give them a menu of ministries to lead and a wide range of responsibilities. Is there any wonder people don't know what's most important? Is there any question as to why we have trouble providing effective evaluation?

Job descriptions filled with hopes and wishes are silly. Effective job descriptions need to reflect reality.

As the leader, you must provide clarity for everyone on your team. It's up to you to make sure everyone is focused on the things that matter most. It comes down to roles and goals. In the next chapter, I'm going to talk about goals, but first let's clarify roles.

If you can help people on your team know what really matters, and what they should do with their time and energy, you're well on your way to leading a focused church.

AREAS OF FOCUS

When you set out to clarify the roles for people on your team, I suggest you start with areas rather than tasks. Recently, I was working with a leader on this very process. Robbie had transitioned from being the worship leader into the executive pastor role. Now this isn't a common transition, but Robbie had the perfect personality for the role.

Since he was new to the job, he hired me to coach him for a few months. He had the skills and the trust, but he wanted some accountability and insight into establishing systems and leading the team. One of the first things we worked on was aligning the staff and getting clear on their roles and goals.

We talked about each person on the team and where he or she provided leadership. We listed the three or four areas where they led and talked about effectiveness. We discussed if they were the right person to lead that area and if it was really important.

Robbie made a simple Excel spreadsheet to guide his discussions. One person oversaw the database, the new member's class, and baptism. Those were his areas of focus. Another part-timer provided leadership to preschool, elementary, and children's check in. Those were her areas of focus. Robbie went down the list and listed every area of ministry in the church, matching it with a leader.

Along the way, we identified several gaps. In some cases, people thought they needed to lead in one area, when in reality they were more valuable in another. In one instance, someone had picked up unnecessary responsibilities and it wasn't the best fit for the team.

Over the course of a few months, Robbie helped everyone move into their sweet spot. Some tasks were taken off people's plates and others were brought front and center. The leadership gap closed and people had clarity around their area of focus in the church. They knew what really mattered and where to focus their energy.

I talked to Robbie a few months after this experience. The church had grown by about 20% and he attributes a big part of that to the team having clarity around their roles. Robbie's job as the Chief Clarity Officer was important and his great leadership had a trickledown effect. He was one of the most coachable leaders I've ever worked with, and his hard work and focus paid off.

EFFECTIVE JOB DESCRIPTIONS

In Chapter 10 we talked about implementing a hiring process. And part of that process was clarifying the position and creating a detailed job profile for a new position.

If you followed that step, the bulk of your work here is already done. When people come on the team, they will have gone through a great process and they should know what's important and what's expected of them.

But what about the existing members of your team? What about people who have muddy job descriptions or no job descriptions at all? If you have someone on your team with no job description, or an out-of-date job description, then it's time to get to work.

Here are some things that should be on everyone's job description:

- » **Primary responsibilities and tasks.** Your goal is not to list every single thing someone *might* do in his or her job. You need to list what they *must* do in order to be successful.

- » **Key performance indicators.** It's amazing how clarity improves when you get honest about what's expected. Key performance indicators are the numbers or metrics used to evaluate success. If I had to guess, I'd say 95% of church job descriptions don't have these.

- » **Personal responsibilities.** Working on staff at a church is different from working just about anywhere else. A good job description will capture some of these personal responsibilities and expectations.

Sit down with everyone and clarify their areas of focus, then drill down into the primary tasks, expectations and responsibilities. If something doesn't need to be on the page, get it off of the page. If something is missing, talk about the gap.

This is the starting point for creating clarity, but the work doesn't stop with one document. A good job description should be reviewed on a regular basis to make sure it's accurate and effective. You should walk through the actual document every time you do an official performance review. We're going to talk about that in Chapter 14.

ONE SENTENCE JOB DESCRIPTION

If you work hard to clarify areas of focus and develop a clear job description for everyone on your staff, you've done far more than most to set people up for success. But there's one more thing you can do in the clarity department.

Every staff member needs a *tweetable* job description; a short bottom line that encapsulates their contribution to the team.

In 2013, Andy Stanley talked about this process at Catalyst. He said one of the most helpful things leaders can do is boil down someone's job into one simple but powerful statement. He says it's time-consuming work, but the results are magic.

Andy shared his one sentence job description. "Inspire our staff and congregations to remain fully engaged in our mission and strategy."

He shared this one, created for the CFO of Northpoint: "Create, implement, and monitor systems that ensure our organization remains fiscally secure."

I absolutely love the one sentence job description created for his administrative assistant: "To keep Andy's path clear of nonessential tasks and decisions so that he can do what only he can do."

Do you see how much focus and clarity comes from knowing the *one thing* that sums up someone's role on the staff team? Once you create these statements, think of how you can continually reinforce them.

As the Chief Clarity officer, it's up to you to provide clarity for everyone on your team. Talk about their area of focus, get serious about a legitimate job description, and fight to encapsulate everything in one tweetable statement. You might find this to be a great project for a staff retreat, but make sure you lead the way.

ACTION STEP

Download the free Staff Clarity Worksheet from churchfuel.com/streamline and use it to guide your clarity work. Your mission is to clarify roles and goals for everyone on your team.

- 12 -

CLARIFY GOALS FOR EVERYONE ON YOUR TEAM

"Once you've established the goals you want and the price you are willing to pay, you can ignore the minor hurts, the opponent's pressure, and the temporary setbacks."

– Vince Lombardi –

When I work with churches, we often start by clarifying and communicating mission, vision, and values. This sometimes frustrates quick-fix seeking pastors who want to see fast results. But I've experienced it time and time again: the groundwork has to come before the harvest. If you don't get organized on the ground level, any tower you build is going to fall.

Once the church knows why it exists (that's the mission) and what it looks like when they get there (that's the vision), you can chart a course (that's the strategy).

And you power all of this with clear goals.

There's tremendous power in setting and working toward goals. That's why I'm a big believer in working as a team to set church-wide annual goals. We're going to talk about a system later.

When everyone on a church staff knows where they're going, there's clarity and alignment and often, success. "You won't do ministry that really matters until you define what matters," says Aubrey Malphurs of The Malphurs Group.

Not only does a church need goals, each person on the staff needs goals for their ministry. Just like church-wide goals keep an organization on track, individual goals will help a team member focus on the right things. Setting goals and keeping them in front of you can make a big difference.

A few years ago, my wife and I set a financial goal to save a certain amount of money to buy a new house. It was a fairly audacious goal, but we knew it was the right thing. I bought a calendar and hung it in my office. My goal was to write a number in a box every day. That number was the amount of "extra" money I made by selling products online. If I sold a $19 product, I'd transfer $19 from my checking account to our designated savings account. Then I'd write $19 in the box for that day.

Some days I didn't sell anything, so I'd just transfer $5 from my regular checking account. Some days, I did much better and the transfer was more significant.

All of these bank transfers might sound silly to you, but performing this action every day and visualizing progress on this wall calendar kept me focused. By the end of the year, we were able to hit our goal. Without this kind of intentionality or focus, I don't believe we would have made it. The goal helped us focus on what we decided was important.

As a leader, one of the most effective management tools at your disposal is helping people set effective goals. Without goals, people will end up responding to the urgent tasks and lose focus on what really matters.

My friend, Matt, once told me that the best way he knows to lead and manage people in a growing church is to help them set goals, then work with them to create a plan to reach those goals, and holding people accountable to reach the goals they set.

DON'T SET THEM...CRAFT THEM

Here's a great question you can ask your staff: "What do you want to see God do in the next year?" Sometimes, you get generic answers. A student pastor might say, "We just want God to show up" or, "We want to see students follow Jesus with their lives." Those are great things.

God is certainly free to do what He wants, but imagine the synergy of casting vision and setting goals around the mission. What would happen if that student pastor set a goal of engaging ten passionate, committed, and trained adult leaders who will lead students to follow Jesus with their lives? The first is a desire. The second is a goal.

Goal setting is more like goal crafting. You should work with people on your team to help them set goals for their ministry. "What do you want to see God do in your ministry and in your leadership?" is a powerful question every leader should ask each person on their team. As you pray and discuss, a preferred vision for the future takes shape. You're free to have conversations rooted in reality about what it's going to take to reach a goal.

It's really important to set goals *with* your team, not for your team. If you hand goals to a team member, they might resent that. Over time, they might get a little passive aggressive, or feel like they're working to accomplish *your* vision. But when you work with someone to set these goals and create a plan to accomplish them, they invite you into the accountability process. You're leading them and holding them accountable in areas where they had input. They won't resent your leadership because you're helping them to accomplish their goals.

SUPPORTING GOALS

When you work with your team to set ministry specific goals, make sure those goals support the church-wide goals. You don't want each ministry setting independent goals or casting a vision that's different from the church. If that happens, you end up with a silo mentality in the church. My friend Tony Morgan talks a lot about the silo mentality (and he does a great job helping churches get out of it, too). He writes:

> One of the common challenges I see in churches that are stuck is that they're operating as many distinct ministries under one roof. In most cases I'm positive they didn't set out to create the situation, but they find themselves in a place where there are ministry silos operating independently from each other.

Each ministry ends up competing with every other ministry for time, attention, space and other resources. I liken this to an unhealthy marriage where the husband and wife are still living in the same house, but they've decided he'll sleep on the couch. There's no unity of purpose.

And, rather than do the hard work of finding a path to heal the marriage relationship, they've decided to live separate lives under the same roof. In both situations, you're just delaying the pain and consequences caused by disunity. And, unfortunately, both dysfunctional environments will eventually negatively impact innocent "family" members.

When you work with your team to set ministry goals, make sure they're the right goals. Make sure they help the ministry succeed, as ministry success translates to church success. If your church is focusing on small group involvement, your student ministry goals should coincide. If your church is working hard to engage in missions, make sure your children's ministry or educational ministries have similar goals.

There's a bit of a science to goal setting, so let's talk about effective goals. Great goals are:

1. **Specific.** "Improve the service" isn't a good goal, because it's not specific. "Recruit three more members for the usher team" is a specific goal. If your church wide priority is to raise the bar on discipleship, how many small group leaders are you going to train? If your church wide priority is to involve more people in generosity, how many new first time donors are you going to reach? If your church wide priority

is to become more intentional with guests, how many first-time guest cards are you going to process this year? When you set goals, make sure they're specific and not generic.

2. **Measurable.** "Do better" or "Get more volunteers" is tough to measure. How many new volunteers do you need to involve? What percentage of total giving do you want to see come in digitally? Write goals that are measurable, so you'll know how you're doing. Goals also need to have a time limit. "Recruit three new volunteers by Easter" is specific and measurable. When you set goals, work hard to make them measurable.

3. **Attainable.** Goals need to challenge and stretch you, but they also need to be realistic. Resist setting unrealistic goals that are thrown out the window as soon as it looks like they won't be reached. Make sure you stretch yourself, but set goals that are within reason.

Does each person on your team have 3-5 specific, measurable, and attainable goals? Do they fit the overall strategy and plan for the church? Are you meeting with them and helping them accomplish them?

ACTION STEP

Set up appointments with each ministry leader to discuss their goals. Put these informal coffee meetings on the calendar then get together to talk about what they want to see God do in their ministries. Use these conversations as the starting point.

- 13 -

CREATE A PERSONALIZED LEADERSHIP DEVELOPMENT PLAN

True self-confidence is the courage to be open—to welcome change and new ideas regardless of their source.

– Carol S. Dweck –

One of my favorite family traditions is Friday night pizza and movie night. We order pizza (or sometimes make our own, which never turn out as good as Pinterest claims) then each kid gets to pick a movie. Depending on who's turn it is, we watch princess movies, ninja movies, or teenage romantic comedies.

But when it's my turn to pick the movie, I go back to the 80s and 90s. These decades produced the best movies in American History.

I want my kids to understand what a flux capacitor is. And it wouldn't be right for me to rob them of experiencing the Mighty

Ducks or to think that Episode 1 fiasco is the true Star Wars. The 80s and 90s were better times—I'm sure of it.

Another one of our traditions is the Sunday night huddle. On Sunday nights, we huddle as a family to talk about the schedule for the upcoming week. It's like a family business meeting. It's hard work to get three kids to the right places at the right times, plus I want them to know about what's going on in mom and dad's world. So we huddle up and talk about everything.

One Sunday night, we started getting stressed with the schedule. Between tests, chorus, baseball, tennis, lacrosse, and two birthday parties, the week looked pretty full. There were a few times when all the kids had to be in different places and there wasn't a way to make it work.

Every family has weeks like this from time to time, but this was becoming normal in our house. The "busy season" was turning into the never-ending season. I know how Mr. Tumness felt when it was always winter and never Christmas.

Our schedule was driving our plans, not the other way around.

We were going with the flow, driving people around, and letting the crazy schedule control us instead of letting an intentional plan dictate our schedule. We were accepting everything as fact and going with the flow, rather than taking charge.

There's nothing wrong with tennis, chorus or lacrosse (though I don't fully understand the rules), but if those activities don't push our family toward our goals, then they're fruitless. We end up doing things just because they're on the schedule, rather than because we really *want* to do them or because they matter.

In that moment, we decided to say no to a "required" chorus meeting and a baseball practice. There were some other things that we decided were more important. And saying no felt good. Besides, five years from now, our kids aren't going to remember that they missed a rehearsal or a practice.

I'm sharing all this family stuff because the principle is true in your church too. Without an intentional plan, you'll spend all of your time responding to things. Opportunities will become obligations. And before you know it, another ministry season will go by without any real change.

THE ACCIDENTAL LEADER

When I talk to pastors and church leaders, most of them tell me they want to be a better leader. Leadership is one of those really important things. I believe it's actually the #1 growth barrier in most churches. It's not style, service times or campuses...it's leadership.

Leadership is like the tide. When it rises, everything else rises with it. If you become a better leader, it will improve every ministry, every program, and every relationship in your church. If everyone in your church learns how to lead better, the entire church will benefit.

Almost all pastors know this. But when I look under the hood, there's nothing on their task list or calendar to back up this claim. The desire is there but the action is absent.

Leadership development is one of those things that will get bumped from your calendar every time. The conference will never be convenient. The book sitting on your desk right now is going to get covered up with other things begging for your time. You won't have time for any of this.

I know it sounds obvious, but you're not going to become a better leader by accident, which is why you *must* do what I'm going to suggest in this chapter.

THERE'S SOMETHING BETTER THAN GOALS

Goals are great. There's a chapter in this book dedicated to helping staff members set goals. You should set annual goals for your church. But goals are actually overrated. There's something far more powerful than goals.

I'm talking about plans.

Goals are great but plans are better. Any knucklehead can set goals. It's working on a plan that makes the difference.

> » There are a lot of people who want to be better parents. That's a great goal, but what's your plan?

> » There are a lot of people who want a better marriage. That's fantastic, but what specifically are you going to do?

> » There are a lot of people who want to get out of debt. Awesome, but what specific behavior are you going to change?

You can have great goals, but without solid plans, you won't accomplish them. You can set a goal to run a marathon, but if you don't have a plan, you'll never accomplish anything. You can set a goal to lose 20 pounds, but if you don't have an eating plan, nothing will change.

Goals are fantastic, but plans are much better.

So when we're talking about becoming a better leader, let's stop talking about desire and opportunity and get serious about what you're going to do. You can't make it a goal to become a better leader or help others on your team become better leaders—you have to create a plan.

NO SHORTAGE OF OPTIONS

There's no shortage of resources at your disposal to help you become a better leader.

A great leader such as Carey Nieuwhof can spend hours arranging guests, conducting interviews and putting together a leadership podcast. With a couple of clicks, I can access this incredible resource for free. He's done all this work and I can listen at no cost. This is amazing. And that's just one of the amazing podcasts available to you for free on the internet.

Simon Sinek can spend two years researching, outlining, and writing an incredible leadership book called *Leaders Eat Last*. I can purchase the final version for less than $20. What took years to write and thousands of dollars to create, I can get for next to nothing. And there are hundreds of other well-researched, well-written, top-quality leadership books. Many of these represent people's life work. For the cost of a couple of meals, you can purchase valuable content that took thousands of hours to create.

Then there are conferences like Leadercast and the Global Leadership Summit. Months of event planning and production go into an event. Hundreds of thousands of dollars are spent on content and I can access it all for a few hundred bucks. Other people have done all the hard work, putting together a program you could never produce on your own, and you can attend.

You know all of this. You've known about these resources and events for some time. And I'm not trying to guilt you into signing up for something.

But I am trying to get you to create a plan to digest some of the content that's available to you. I am trying my best to get you to be intentional and make some decisions. Growth is not going to happen by accident. Plans are not going to appear out of thin air.

So take out a sheet of paper or open up a new document. Call it a Leadership Development Plan. Write one for yourself and work with everyone on your team to create one as well.

WHAT GOES ON THE PLAN?

Write down the two or three things you want to improve as a leader. Then start writing down what you're going to do to make it happen. You're not writing down desires or goals, you're writing down plans.

Write down the specific names of books you're going to read, people you're going to meet, and events you're going to attend. Decide in advance when you're going to do these things as you write down your plan. Here are some things you can include on your leadership development plan:

» **Podcasts.** If you want to improve as a preacher, decide to listen to one podcast a week. Go ahead and write down the name of the podcast and the people you're going to learn from. There are podcasts on every topic imaginable, but decide what you're going to do right now.

» **Books.** Ask friends for recommendations, but decide what books you're going to read. Books are my favorite leadership development tool because the bar is often higher. Reputable authors and books are well-researched and go through a vetting process. Blogs are great, but books are better. Decide how many you're going to read and list their titles. Assign each book to a season of the year or a month on the calendar. Then order them all and place them on your desk.

» **Conferences.** As a leader, you should attend one or two conferences every year. I know they're expensive and travel is required, but they're worth it. Look at the next 12 months and decide what you're going to attend. Put it on your calendar and make travel reservations. Buy your conference tickets and book your hotel room. I promise that something will come up at the church that will make it a "bad time to be gone," but stick to your plan.

» **Conversations.** Great leaders understand that there's a wealth of information to be gained from relationships. Are there people you want to connect with or learn from as a part of your leadership development? Write their names down and make a plan to get them coffee or buy them lunch. Maybe you can put together an informal meeting of a small group of leaders to talk about a specific leadership topic. These conversations or informal groups can be a tremendous asset to you.

» **Coaching.** "Picking people's brains" is great, but some of the best leaders I know pay money to be a part of a formal coaching program. There's something about *paying* a coach and joining other people on a similar process. Whether it's online or in person, there are tons of great coaching groups available to you. Don't be a victim of broke thinking and say you can't afford this. Find a way, because a great education is worth it.

Your leadership development plan is unique to you. If you're not a reader, don't load it up with books. If you learn best in conference environments, lean heavily there. Write a real plan for becoming a better leader.

And when you're done with your plan, sit down with each person on your team to create one for them. If you have someone that wants to become a better communicator, work with them to create a plan. If there's someone on your staff who wants to grow as a leader, work with them to create a specific plan.

ACTION STEP

Create your own personalized leadership development plan.
It would be great if everyone on your team had one,
but start with yourself. Remember, leaders always go first.
You can download a free Word document template
from churchfuel.com/streamline.

- 14 -

SCHEDULE PERFORMANCE EVALUATIONS

Success comes to those who habitually do things that unsuccessful people don't do.

– John Maxwell –

Creating clarity is one of the most important jobs for any leader.

But it's not enough to create clarity; you must continually fight for it. You see, the tendency in any organization is to drift. You drift from the mission, lured away by good opportunities that "mostly" fit. You drift from your passion, tempted to pursue less important things. You drift from key decisions, allowing everyday pressures to lull you into an acceptance of the current reality.

In the wake of overwhelming opportunity and endless mission, it's really hard to stay focused.

But in order for your staff to lead well, they need *you* to lead well. They need you to fight through all of the programs, ministries, and opportunities that exist in a growing church and help them focus on the things they must do well. They need you to help them stay focused.

ROLES AND GOALS MUST BE CONTINUALLY REVIEWED.

A new team member comes to their job with incredible focus and passion. They're excited about their ministry and their job description makes sense. They dive into the work and start meeting people. After a few months, the passion is still there but their role becomes unclear. They pick up other responsibilities and head off in a few different directions. Good things take them away from great things. Opportunities become obligations. And their passion begins to wane.

That's why you have to sit down and have re-focusing conversations. I recommend a scheduled, formal evaluation every six months.

PEOPLE NEED TO KNOW HOW THEY ARE DOING.

I've heard from many employees who thought things were going well, until a sudden conversation changed their entire outlook. When conversations are honest, surprises should be rare.

It's hard to be honest and dive deep in a ten-minute performance review or a hallway conversation. The goal isn't to check a box and put a document in the employee file. And while an open door policy is great, if you don't sit down for an extended period of time after adequate preparation from both parties, you're missing the point of an evaluation. You can go through the motions and never see the benefit.

Not only does your staff need to know how they're doing, great employees *want* to know how they're doing. The chances are that your people desire feedback and crave clarity. Give it to them because they can handle the truth.

EFFECTIVENESS MUST BE EVALUATED.

Churches need leaders who perform at a high level. Don't let that word scare you. Christianity is not about performance. God loves you, accepts you and blesses you out of His good will, not because of anything you've done. You've been saved by grace and it's a complete and free gift.

And while the gospel of grace should permeate everything in a church, we cannot discount the need to be good stewards in our jobs. You cannot coast through ministry because you're a good Christian or a nice person. You need to do your job, and you need to do it well.

That's why you have to get beyond the fact that your team is full of nice people who love Jesus. You've got to evaluate how well they do their job.

A PERFORMANCE REVIEW IS COACHING, NOT CRITICISM.

If you want to develop people, you must learn to be a coach, not a critic. A critic says, "I didn't like that." A coach says, "Here's why this didn't work the way you probably hoped." A critic says to the worship pastor, "I didn't like that song." A coach says, "That was a great song, but I'm not sure it fit at the beginning of the worship set because…" A critic says, "That wasn't a good sermon." A coach says, "You might have lost the audience in the middle because it was information heavy…I think people would have benefited from a story there."

Critics tend to be ignored, while people generally crave coaching. Make sure you let your staff know how they're doing along the way, and coach them on how they can do things better.

So let's talk about the performance review and how it should work.

When I work with churches on setting up a leadership structure, I help them clarify roles and goals for each person on their team. We build org charts and create leadership rhythms that can sustain growth. And I recommend they implement official performance reviews every six months.

Twice a year, have a scheduled, lengthy, and in-depth conversation about performance, expectations, and roles. Both parties should prepare for this conversation, and it should be documented. I recommend an evaluation form with letter grades. There are lots of ways to grade people but I've been getting letter grades since the 2nd grade at Hendricks Avenue Elementary School and it's a system everyone understands.

If you're looking for a template, you can download one for free at churchfuel.com/streamline. This is the actual evaluation form I use.

Here are seven things you should rate at each performance review:

1. **Core Values.** If your church has core values, the first thing you should rate is how well each person reflects them in their life and work. If "excellence" is a core value, how

excellent is this person's work? If "creativity" is a core value, how creative are they on a weekly basis?

2. **Quality of Work.** When evaluating quality of work, you've got to set aside personality and friendship. You should never fully separate leadership from relationship, but you can't let the relationship keep you from being their leader. Keep the grade (and the subsequent conversation) focused on facts and performance.

3. **Dependability.** This is one of the things I always evaluate with team members because I want to be able to count on people no matter what. When you assign a letter grade, you'll want to talk about specific examples.

4. **Relational Skills.** People can't really lead in a church from behind their desk or through their email program. So be honest about their relational skills. How well do they work with their leaders and peers? How well do they interact with volunteers and church members?

5. **Communication.** Not every communicator is a leader, but every leader must be a great communicator. How clear is this person? Do they get their point across in email or in training meetings? Are they prepared? Are they effective?

6. **Stewardship.** If this person manages money, how well do they do it? How well do they leverage church resources? It's not just about being frugal; it's about being wise.

7. **Growth.** Is this person growing as a leader? Are they learning from others who are ahead of them, reading books or attending conferences? You can evaluate all you want, but if someone doesn't take steps to learn, then little

change will happen. That's why evaluating personal growth should be a part of your conversation.

Those are seven categories I evaluate, but you can add, delete, or change things on this list. The important thing is to think through what you want to evaluate for each person. Lock it down and create a performance review form. Use the same form for every employee and every meeting. It might be awkward the first time, but the more you do it, the easier it will get.

ASK QUESTIONS

In addition to giving scores for categories, you'll want to ask several open ended questions. The real goal of an evaluation isn't to record grades on a form for the employee file, it's to create meaningful conversations that lead to greater effectiveness. It's an opportunity to be a great leader and develop the leadership potential in someone else.

That's why performance reviews should encourage conversations and feedback. People need the opportunity to talk about their work experiences in their own words. Your job as a leader is to get them to open up. You must create a culture where people are not punished for honesty.

Here are some great questions to use in the second half of the performance evaluation meeting:

1. **What do you love about your job right now?** When people are working in their sweet spot, it doesn't feel like work. People don't burn out and become ineffective over time when they truly care about what they are doing. So dig deep and press for specifics.

2. **What part of your job don't you enjoy?** Everyone has things on their job description that they don't love. In some cases, you might find people struggle with something that isn't critical to their role or job description. Perhaps they have picked up other responsibilities they don't need and consequently feel under pressure.

3. **What is most difficult right now?** People often know their areas of struggle, so give them the opportunity to talk about their difficulties. Don't let it turn into a gripe session, but listen and advise.

4. **Where do you need me more and where do you need me less?** As a leader, this is one of my favorite questions to ask people on my team. It gives them permission to open up and talk about me. That means I need to shut up and listen. Sometimes, your staff needs you more. They might need more direction or clarity. They might ask for your physical presence in their environments. They might need more resources. Listen to what they're saying and don't shut them down. At other times, they may need you less. If they're a leader, they might feel like you're micromanaging or offering too many critiques. The more you ask this question, the more honest they will be.

5. **What actions do you need to take in the next six months?** Evaluations that don't lead to actions are useless. You can have a great conversation with someone, but without an action plan, change won't happen. That's why it's important to end the performance review by creating a specific plan of action for the next six months.

ACTION STEP

Your homework for this chapter is to schedule performance evaluations. You don't have to conduct them, just schedule the. You could set aside a week as "Performance Review Week"—put it on the master calendar and make sure everyone does a performance evaluation with their supervisor. Download a staff evaluation form (along with five other evaluation forms) at churchfuel.com/forms.

- 15 -

IMPLEMENT A TEAM MEETING SYSTEM

An organization's ability to learn, and translate that learning into action rapidly, is the ultimate competitive advantage.

- Jack Welch -

Do your meetings lead to a lot of talk and only a little action?

Have you ever sat through a meeting and thought, "Why am I here?"

If you send an email to your team saying the next staff meeting is optional, how many people will attend?

Most team meetings aren't effective because they don't focus on what's important. You rarely have time to talk about the mission, vision, values, and long-term strategy because you're responding to what happened last week. You don't spend much time talking about how to improve the church service (something everyone experiences) because you're responding to last week's crisis (something that affects a handful of people).

I've worked with churches for more than two decades. My first church job was in youth ministry at a small church in Tallahassee, Florida, and I spent more than a decade working with teenagers. From there, I became a church planter and senior pastor. All of this means I've sat through and led countless meetings. Some of them were great, but most of them were ineffective.

A few years ago, I participated in a coaching experience with several entrepreneurs and business leaders. My business partner and I learned so much from this multi-million dollar company, and the conversational coaching environment was perfect for where we were as an organization. We talked about systems, strategies, and vision. But one of the biggest takeaways was a meeting system.

This particular company had been using the meeting system for years, having learned it themselves from a book called *Mastering the Rockefeller Habits*. It was brand new to us, but it made complete sense. We came home and implemented our version right away. We got better at it and it became a part of our culture. After a couple of years, we could point to this single change as one of the biggest catalysts for our growth.

Here's an overview of the system, with some thoughts on how it might work in your church.

START WITH AN ANNUAL RETREAT

It's important to look at the meeting system as a whole, with all the puzzle pieces fitting together to form one picture. Each part of the meeting system sets the tone for the next part. They build on each other, and fit together perfectly.

The Annual Retreat is a three day, two night retreat focused on annual planning. This is a big deal, and getting away from the routine of the week is critical to stepping back and looking at the church as a whole.

Take the first day of your annual retreat and look back. Don't rush this because looking back and understanding the previous year is a key to setting the tone for the next year. When you look back, here are some things you'll want to cover:

» Review the numbers. You might want to have someone prepare a report and share with the group.

» Talk about wins and losses. What went well and what didn't go well last year? Spend a good bit of time here and allow people to talk.

» Talk about last year's goals. Did you meet them? Did you fall short? Why or why not?

» Talk about lessons learned. As someone shares a lesson, let them expand on it. Try to capture the essence of that lesson in a memorable statement.

Your goal is not to get through this section as fast as possible in order to continue with the planning. Instead, take your time and really explore the past year.

On the second day of your retreat, look forward. Your goal is to come up with three to five annual priorities—big, church-wide things you should accomplish in the next year. These annual priorities will make your church better, and they probably sit just outside of your normal church week. In other words, for these things to happen, it's going to take focus and energy from the whole team.

You'll eventually get down to three to five priorities, but start with brainstorming a list. Let people throw out things they believe are worthy of church-wide focus in the coming year. Keep brainstorming until you've put everything on the whiteboard and then start whittling them down. To get you thinking in the right direction, here are some examples of good annual priorities:

- » Focus on reaching first-time guests.

- » Increase the temperature of generosity in our church.

- » Raise the bar on leadership.

- » Discover and define our mission and vision.

- » Create systems and strategies to calm the chaos.

Each of these objectives is big. They require every staff member and cut across every ministry. Reaching first-time guests can involve children, students, and adults. Raising the bar on leadership is a church-wide objective.

Even though your objectives are church-wide, every objective should be assigned a champion. This is one of the biggest mistakes I see churches make with objectives. Without *one* clear leader to keep the objective on focus, it will flounder. So appoint a person who will push this objective throughout the year.

The second part of looking forward is setting goals. As you look to the coming year, where do you want to end? What's the target?

Don't skip this step, because if you don't talk about the results you want to see, you only have dreams. You can't get *there* if you don't know where *there* is. But if you take the time to clarify your goals, you'll keep you and your team from drifting. In a little while, you'll see how these goals will come back throughout the year and facilitate focus.

You might find it helpful to create a category of goals you use each year. You might choose attendance, giving, group involvement, mission trips, first time guests, and a few other categories. Every year that you hold the annual retreat, you'll review results and set new goals.

When I teach this system, one of the questions I always get is, "Who should be at this meeting?" While it's different for each church, I can give you a few principles and best practices:

1. **Invite forward thinkers who don't get stressed out when talking in abstract.** You want strategic people in your strategic meetings, and there's nothing more strategic than charting the course for the next year. It might be a little uncomfortable to change, but a person's title or position should not determine their involvement in this kind of meeting.

2. **Invite people who care about the church as a whole.** If the youth pastor can't put the good of the church above the good of the student ministry, she's not going to be helpful in this kind of meeting. I'd say that's a bigger problem, but

we'll save that discussion for later. When you're talking about the direction of the church, it's important to think church before ministry.

That's the annual retreat—the one time a year where you review the past year and look toward the next one. But the meeting system is about to get much more powerful and practical.

STAY FOCUSED WITH THE QUARTERLY RETREAT

Church objectives and church goals are great. But if these live in a document and don't reappear for months at a time, they won't make much of a difference. Your entire annual retreat will retroactively turn into an exercise in futility without a systematic process for staying focused.

That's where the quarterly retreat comes in. It's a miniature version of the annual retreat, where you take your objectives and goals and talk about what you're going to do this quarter to make it happen. In my opinion, this quarterly retreat is the secret sauce of this system.

I've seen a lot of churches conduct annual planning retreats only to lose focus and energy halfway through the year. But if you do this step, you'll connect your big picture annual plans to real life in your church.

The quarterly retreat is one night and two days long. It's a little bit shorter, but it's more focused and practical. Begin with looking back on the last quarter, much like you did at the annual retreat. This will naturally go faster because you're covering less ground. Next, look ahead to the next quarter.

The power comes from taking our annual objectives and assigning a quarterly priority. Essentially, take one big goal and break it down into something you can accomplish in one quarter. Here are some examples:

» Let's say your goal is to focus on reaching guests in the next year. Well, what can you totally accomplish in the next three months to make significant progress on this objective? What can you check off in the next three months? Maybe this is the quarter when you research what's working at other churches you respect. That's one important step you can fully take.

» If your annual objective is to raise the bar on leadership, maybe your quarterly priority this quarter should be to clarify roles and goals for all of your existing leaders. Your point person can drive the project and everyone can contribute to the process.

» If your annual objective is to increase generosity among your members, maybe this is the quarter you plan a generosity retreat or implement a thank you campaign. It's one of four important steps that will lead you where you want to go.

Every annual objective gets four quarterly steps. They're smaller and more specific. And most importantly, you can fully accomplish them in one quarter.

Imagine the focus your team will have knowing what you're going to accomplish in the coming months, and that those accomplishments are part of a larger objective that really matters.

CONTINUE WORKING WITH A MONTHLY MEETING

There's a tremendous power in the meeting and retreat system, and it gets better and better the more you use it. It's powerful because the system allocates actual meeting time to the big things that you have decided are the most important. Without this system, you'll respond to short-term problems and never move the ball down the field. With this system, you'll create intentional times where you discuss important issues with the right people.

So let's keep drilling down. The monthly meeting is the third part of this meeting system.

Once a month, spend one day focusing on the quarterly objective. So, we've taken our annual objective and broken it down to a quarterly priority. Now we're taking a day and working on implementing our quarterly priority. It's how you stay focused on what's important. It's how you make progress on your goals. Here are some things you might discuss during your one day monthly meeting:

» **Review the numbers.** You might find it helpful to create a pretty report that shows where you are in relation to your goals. Most people don't like spreadsheets and don't understand pictures. We turned the final part of our financial report into a smiley face or a sad face.

» **Give updates on quarterly priorities.** Each point person should give an update on their quarterly priority. Talk about what's been done and what still needs to be done. Get input on decisions and next steps.

» **Talk about one or two "big rocks."** That language comes from the *Mastering the Rockefeller Habits* book I mentioned at the start of the chapter. But the idea is to talk about one or two things that involve everyone, not just a bunch of random stuff that could be decided elsewhere. Keep your big rocks related to your quarterly priorities. If your annual priority is to get guest friendly and your quarterly objective was to evaluate three other churches, your big rock discussion might be what you should implement and what you should avoid from each of your model churches. The key with the big rock discussion is *preparation*. Make sure everyone knows what's being discussed and insist everyone come prepared.

You can probably do your monthly meeting at the church—there's no need to go away. And some churches might be able to accomplish everything in half a day, or three quarters of a day.

Remember the principles of calendar planning we talked about in the first four chapters? Your annual, quarterly, and monthly meeting dates should go on your master calendar. Let them become a part of your natural rhythm.

THE WEEKLY MEETING IS MOSTLY CALENDAR AND COMMUNICATION

The final part of the meeting system is probably the part most familiar to churches because it looks like a lot of church staff meetings. Even with the annual priorities, quarterly objective and monthly meeting, you still probably need a time to check in and talk about what's going on.

There's a lot of flexibility with this meeting, but here are a few best practices:

> » Keep your annual priorities, quarterly objectives, and church-wide goals in front of people constantly. Print them on the top of every agenda so you don't lose sight of what's most important.

> » Make sure someone covers the calendar and important communication. Maybe you print dates and information on the agenda and give people the opportunity to ask questions and seek clarity. "A breakdown in communication" is one of the most popular reasons people give for missing the mark on something, so with a standing meeting on the calendar you've got a great opportunity to get this right.

> » Share stories and learn from each other. Many churches take the first part of their weekly meeting to share stories from the life of the church. This is a great practice because it helps keep it real. You might also discover the people in the meeting have incredible insights to share with the rest of the group. Consider giving them 20 minutes to share what

God is doing in their life or report on something they're learning as a leader.

The meeting system is a powerful way to ensure you're talking about the most important stuff throughout the year and not just during the strategic planning retreat. It's a great way to connect the dots, and align your calendar and your team around church-wide objectives.

ACTION STEP

This was a pretty heavy chapter with a lot of moving parts.
It's easy to get lost in the weeds and miss the overall point.
Download and watch a free training video on this meeting rhythm.
It will walk you through each type of meeting and
give you more examples. You can watch with your team and decide if it's
right for you. Download the video for free at churchfuel.com/streamline.

- 16 -

WRITE VOLUNTEER JOB DESCRIPTIONS

I'm convinced that the influence a church has on its community will be determined in large part not by the personality of the pastor, the size of its building or how long the ministry has worked in the community. It will be determined instead by the percentage of involvement in the ministry of each member.

– Wayne Cordeiro –

The Apostle Paul says it's the job of the pastors and elders to equip people to do the work of the ministry.

Yet in many churches, it's the church that pays a professional to do the work of the ministry. Boards hire pastors to visit the sick, preach the Word, and lead ministries. And while there's nothing wrong with those things, the presence of paid staff doesn't absolve the members from doing the work of the ministry.

If you're depending on paid staff to do everything, you're in big trouble because you will never be able to hire enough people to get it all done. There will always be the need for qualified, committed staff members, but if you want to reach your full potential, you will need to involve volunteers.

God designed the church this way.

In the Old Testament, it was the work of the priest to stand before God on behalf of the people. God outlined particular requirements for priests, right down to their dress code. In the New Testament, things changed. The author of Hebrews describes Jesus as the great high priest, the once-and-for-all sacrifice for the sins of the world. Peter says in his first epistle that Christians are a royal priesthood. Paul says our bodies are temples of the Holy Spirit.

In other words, the church doesn't have a priest; the church is full of priests. It's not up to highly qualified, highly trained, highly educated super-Christians to do all of the work of the ministry. Ministry is done by the priesthood, by the body of Christ using their spiritual gifts to build up the church.

Every Christian in your church is like a priest, called to serve somewhere. People may not know it, and they might need training, but they have a crucial part in your church's mission. God's plan is not for a small band of superheroes to do everything in the church, but for a team of people to build an army of servant leaders who share the gospel with the world.

So your role as the Chief Clarity Officer doesn't stop with your staff. It extends to every volunteer who serves. You must help people discover their gifts and find a place to use them. It's not just good leadership. It's a command.

Lots of good things will happen when you have healthy volunteers. But the biggest benefit is that the church will grow. As a church leader, you can only do so much. You can't lead all the ministries or talk to all the people. You cannot do it all.

But when volunteers understand the mission and vision of the church, and are empowered to serve and lead, and they do so in the right areas, a powerful thing happens. The church gets healthy and it grows in size *at the same time*. Working on your volunteer ministry really does lead to church health and church growth.

VOLUNTEER BURNOUT

Tell me if this sounds familiar...

A family comes to your church from another church. They were active members but they seem to have left on good terms. They're excited about the mission, vision, and sense of life at your church and they're excited to dive in.

They join a small group and after a few weeks they decide to host the weekly gathering at their home. Since they have a teenager, they get involved in the Wednesday night student program. At first, they're just a positive presence, but before long, they're leading a group.

He's asked to go on the high school campout. She's asked to coordinate food for the DNOW. They both say yes. In staff meetings, their names come up as potential solutions to all kinds of problems.

They're happy volunteers and committed givers for a year or two, but then the wheels start to rattle. Almost without warning, they disappear for a few weeks. They come back for a week or two but then they go dark again.

When you're finally able to coordinate schedules, they tell you they're burned out. It turns out their last church experience didn't end as smoothly as you thought, and they now feel like they need a break. There's nothing wrong and nothing bad happened, but it all feels different.

This is the nice version of the story. It's entry-level burnout. In churches all across the country, the waves are much, much bigger. While you may not be able to totally eliminate volunteer burnout, you can drastically reduce it.

PREVENTING BURNOUT

As a pastor, it's your job to protect your flock from burnout. It's not good for them and it's not good for the church. It's not okay to accept this as a part of ministry. You must take intentional steps to encourage and equip your leaders.

You need healthy volunteer systems to appreciate and communicate with your volunteers. This isn't complicated. It's as simple as deciding to do something for your volunteers every month. Maybe it's an inspirational email one month and a handwritten note the next month. Maybe it's a leadership gathering where people have a good time. Maybe it's mailing them a book or asking how you can pray for them specifically. If you put some thought and creativity into this, you could come up with a powerful list of 12 ways to encourage your volunteers.

But I want to take you back to the beginning—the moment when someone decided to get involved in a new way. When new volunteers come on the team, one of the most important things you can do is provide clarity.

Sometimes, volunteers burn out because they're doing things they should never have been doing in the first place. They take on more stuff because they love the church and love saying yes. And let's be honest—you're grateful there's someone else leading.

But when people serve in areas outside of their calling or away from their sweet spot, they're beginning the slow fade to burnout. Volunteers who serve all over the place are at a greater risk of burnout than leaders who focus their energy on one ministry.

Just like you have to fight for clarity on your staff, you must fight for clarity for your volunteers. Whether it's you or another ministry leader, someone needs to protect them from biting off more than they can chew. They need clear roles and responsibilities, as well as the inspiration to stay focused on what really matters.

WHAT'S THE SOLUTION?

Every volunteer and leader in your church needs a short and clear job description. Like most of the systems I'm discussing in this book, this one is simple but very powerful.

If you want to get on the same page with your volunteers, create an actual page. Open up a new document and write down the details of their position. Your volunteers will appreciate the clarity and you'll help set them up for success.

What kind of things should go on this short job description? Every volunteer job description should contain the following:

» The name of the position.

» How much time it takes. Is this two hours every Sunday? Does it require two to three hours of prep time during the week? Be honest with people and let them know how much time they'll need to invest to be successful. Your goal is not to switch people into serving, luring them into the promise of ease, and then dumping fresh time commitments on them once they're in.

» How long they will serve? Volunteers shouldn't be asked to make life-long commitments. In most cases, six months or one year is the right time frame. That will break down some of the barriers to entry. In some cases, you may need volunteers to commit to a longer term of service. Either way, be clear.

» The name and contact information for their direct leader. Just like staff members have supervisors and bosses, volunteers need to know who they should talk to if there's an issue. Plus, if you let people know who to call if they have a problem, they won't always call *you*.

» Four or five bullet points detailing the specific responsibilities. You don't need to write down dozens of things, but describe the role. Write down what tasks people will perform and what responsibilities they have.

The clearer you can be with volunteers, the happier they will be. And since your ministry probably runs off volunteers, having a happy and fulfilled volunteer base should be a top priority.

FOCUSED JOB DESCRIPTIONS

People in volunteer leadership roles in the church often operate with assumptions based on past experience, so they end up doing things that aren't truly helpful. In most cases, they don't overstep their boundaries or underperform in their responsibilities because they're *bad* people, but because there aren't clearly written and communicated expectations.

Not long ago, I worked with a pastor to help create a volunteer system in their church. In addition to creating new teams to welcome guests, we worked on clarifying the role of some of the existing leaders.

This particular church had a stewardship team, and while there was a job description in the church bylaws, it wasn't clear or helpful. The team met once a month and looked at reports. They talked about expenses and giving during their meetings. And once a year, they created and approved the general church budget.

When I talked to the pastor, he expressed a desire to have this team more involved in the fundraising process. "What good does it do for them to get together and review past reports?" he asked, with a frustrated tone in his voice. "The people on this team have never gotten proactive about raising the temperature of giving in our church," he continued. Finally, he admitted this: "Two of the five people on the stewardship team don't even tithe to the church."

This is a tremendous opportunity to create clarity through creating (or recreating) a job description for each person on the stewardship team. After all, it's tough for people to meet unwritten expectations.

If you want the stewardship team to get involved in funding, not just reporting, that's something you've got to talk about on the front end. That's something that needs to be written on their job description, and people need to understand it before they agree to serve. Personal generosity is an expectation that needs to be communicated in advance. It should go right on the job description.

If you want to get on the same page with people, create an actual page. Move your thoughts out of your head and onto a sheet of paper. A lot of times, leaders get frustrated when volunteers don't meet their expectations. Clarifying those expectations with a written job description is the first step in eliminating this confusion.

If you need Sunday School teachers to come to four training meetings each year, put that on the job profile. Better yet, put the actual dates and times of the training on the job description and make sure people know it in advance.

If you need greeters and ushers to get to church 30 minutes before the service starts, make sure that's written on a sheet of paper and properly communicated.

If you expect deacons to attend the annual deacons retreat or children's workers to send birthday cards, document it on a volunteer job description.

ACTION STEP

Create or update a job description for five key volunteers in your church. You don't have to give one to every person yet—just start with five roles. Write the job description and give them to each volunteer. You can download a free template at churchfuel.com/streamline.

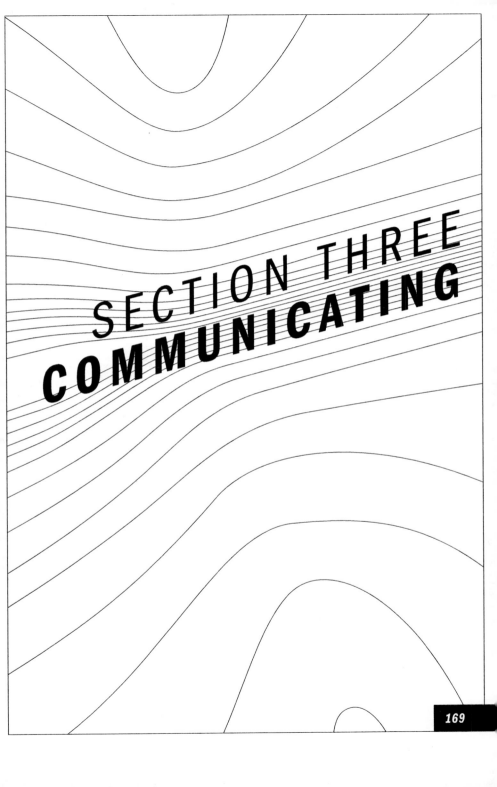

SECTION THREE
COMMUNICATING

- 17 -

HUDDLE WITH VOLUNTEERS EVERY WEEK

Intelligence is the capacity to receive, decode and transmit information efficiently. Stupidity is blockage of this process at any point.

- Robert Anton Wilson -

What's the best way to communicate important information to volunteers?

Training meetings are great, but everyone can't attend. Email is simple, but 70% of email is unopened and unread. Phone calls take a lot of time and there's really no practical way for you to connect with everyone on an individual basis.

There's probably not a silver bullet, but we tried something that worked really well. Every Sunday we gathered volunteers in each department for a short volunteer huddle.

A volunteer huddle is a 10-15 minute "meeting" that happens before every service. Production, Guest Service, and Children's Ministry teams gathered in their respective groups for a pre-game pep talk.

We still had training meetings and we still sent emails, but these Sunday morning volunteer huddles quickly became one of our most important communication points.

CONSTANT VISION CASTING

Churches work hard to craft mission and vision statements only to relegate them to the "about us" page on a website. Crafting a vision statement is one thing; communicating it is something entirely different.

Your volunteers need to be reminded of the mission (why your church exists) and the vision (where your church is going) over and over again. You might feel like they're sick of you talking about it, but just when you think you're about to sound like a broken record that's the moment most people *begin* to understand.

Not only do your volunteers need to hear the mission and vision of the church, you must constantly explain how what they do every week fits with the overall mission. They need to know that what they do really matters. You must continually cast vision, both corporately and personally.

A volunteer huddle is a great time to do this, and you can do it 52 times a year. And 52 mini vision talks beats your "About Us" page every time.

SPOT TRAINING

Do you struggle to get volunteers to specialized training meetings? Even though you know they're important and you communicate tremendous value, I bet quite a few don't make the meetings and miss out on the valuable information.

However, every weekend these volunteers show up early at church, ready to lead and ready to serve. Since they're already there, that's the perfect time to communicate vision and deliver quick bursts of training.

There's a time and a place for extended training, but why not capitalize on the weekend when people are already planning to show up? Why not piggyback on their presence and carve out a few moments to provide weekly training?

When you gather all your volunteers for a weekly huddle, you can do three or four minutes of training on specific issues. You can talk with your greeters about how to recognize someone who needs a handshake. You can share a tip for how to calm a nervous child. You can remind people what they need to put away as they leave their rooms. Spot training like this is very effective because it's timely. People can learn something bite-size and immediately put it into practice.

SUCCESS STORIES

When Jesus wanted to make a point, He told a story.

That's how I coach pastors who are working on their sermons. Too many times we rely on more information to make our point. Yet everything from science to psychology to Scripture tells us that stories are far more effective.

So when you gather your volunteers for a short huddle, make sure you're giving enough time to storytelling. Ask people to share what God is doing in their lives. Let people talk about what happened last week. If you get people talking and sharing, stories will shape the culture of your teams for the better.

A SIMPLE FORMULA FOR A WEEKLY VOLUNTEER HUDDLE

Here's a simple agenda you can follow when you gather your volunteers together for a weekly huddle. Staff members and key volunteers can use the VIP acronym to guide these huddles.

» **Vision.** Every week, remind volunteers why they're serving. Share a win, tell a story, or explain the mission of the church. It's important to continually remind people of the *why behind the what.*

» **Information.** Share important information with the team, from things they need to know for that day to mini-training modules. Talk to your kid's leaders about the bathroom policy. Talk to greeters about how to deal with disruptive guests. Each week, pick a different topic and explain it. This is where you do your mini-training.

» **Prayer.** Spend a few minutes praying for the morning. Pray for the other volunteers. Pray for the pastor and the worship team. Occasionally, ask people if they have special concerns and pray for each other. It will require some education on your part, and you'll have to stick to your guns, but a Volunteer Huddle before each service is an effective way to engage your volunteer.

ACTION STEP

Try a VIP Huddle this week.
You don't have to plan it for every week—
just try it once and see how it feels.

- 18 -

GATHER ALL YOUR LEADERS QUARTERLY

The single biggest problem in communication is the illusion that it has taken place.

- George Bernard Shaw -

I grew up in a conservative Baptist Church.

I attended church on Sunday morning, Sunday night, and Wednesday night. On Tuesday nights during my high school years, we met at McDonalds before heading out on Visitation, which was essentially showing up unannounced at people's homes to tell them about Jesus. On Saturdays in the fall, we gathered at the church from 10am to 4pm for a program called "Discipleship." It was all good though because if we completed the discipleship program, we got a free ski trip.

On spring break, we went on choir tour, singing at youth revivals and rallies up and down the East coast. We all felt like choir boy rock stars on tour busses.

There were unwritten rules about going to prom, but no worries, our church held a formal banquet at the end of the year that served as a mildly entertaining alternative. "Who are you asking to the banquet?" was the same as, "Who are you taking to prom?"

My church didn't have to work hard to convince me to participate. I was there every time the doors were open.

When I read about these events in the church bulletin or newsletter (those were the days before email and social media), they would use words like "food, fellowship, and fun." I saw this combination of alliterated words hundreds of times.

» Come to the Thursday night Bible study because there will be food, fellowship, and fun.

» Don't forget to sign up for the camping trip. It's food, fellowship, and fun.

» VBS is next week. There will be food, fellowship, and tons of fun for 1st to 5th graders.

I don't know if the people writing these announcements weren't really trying, or if we were all really motivated by the 3 F's of Baptist announcements.

After I graduated from high school, I went to college at Florida State University. I became the youth pastor at Lakeview Baptist Church, where I organized tons of events that promised food, fellowship, and fun.

OUR OWN VERSION OF FOOD, FELLOWSHIP, AND FUN

When I became a church planter in 2005, I realized these alliterated benefits weren't going to work on adults. It was time to step things up. I stopped using the word "fellowship" and changed it to community. This sounded far more grown up and less like a room for Wednesday night supper. We had enough trouble getting the attention of serious people, so I decided to drop "fun" as well.

We had to be more creative in our communication. But we found another environment for food, fellowship, and fun in our brand new church plant. And it turned out to be my favorite church activity ever.

Four times a year, we invited every volunteer, donor, and leader to something we called a Leadership Summit. It was as creatively named as the aforementioned Discipleship program on Saturdays, but hey...it worked.

The very first Leadership Summit was basically worship and teaching, but there was something powerful about a gathering of the core leaders of the church. There was a feeling in the room which we didn't have on Sunday mornings. There was time for conversations—time we didn't have on Sunday mornings. There really was fellowship and fun. All that was missing was food.

We fixed that the next quarter, adding a light dinner to the mix, and then the event became a regular part of our program. Today, I recommend that every church gather their leaders once a quarter. Call it something more creative if you wish, but don't miss the opportunity to gather, inspire, and hang out with key leaders in your church.

Let me break down what we did each time we gathered.

WE PROVIDED CHILDCARE

If we're going to ask all of our volunteers and leaders to come to the church building for a time of inspiration, we knew we needed to provide childcare. In fact, every time we asked people to come to this meeting, we made it a priority to take care of their children. It's tough for parents of children, and this makes it a little easier. If you need to have a meeting and you can't afford to provide childcare, I'd reconsider.

We asked another local church to provide childcare for this event so none of our children's workers needed to serve. The point was to inspire them, not create another environment for them to work. We returned the favor for this church, and it became a nice relationship.

WE ORDERED FOOD

The goal of gathering our volunteers wasn't necessarily training (although some of that happened). We wanted to create conversations. We wanted to give people time to hang out. Food helps this process. Again, this costs money, but if you want your volunteers and leaders to participate, make it easy for them. They're investing their free time into serving, so ordering pizza or setting up a taco bar is the least you can do.

OUR BAND LED WORSHIP

We did a little bit of worship at the Leadership Summit every time we gathered and our people loved this. The band led some of the church favorites. They didn't need to practice since they were the greatest hits. And since our volunteers didn't have to do anything, they were free to worship. The room had a great vibe and our worship team loved leading.

WE GAVE AN AWARD OR TWO

This was my favorite part of the evening. Each time we gathered, I'd give one or two awards to volunteers who were doing an awesome job. We paid to create some custom, metal awards and gave them out like the Grammys. When we got to this segment of the evening, we played it up, talking about this person but holding back their name. We asked their co-workers and family members for stories and we bragged on them in front of everyone. When we finally called their name, they'd get a standing ovation.

Figure 5. One of the metal "Leafy Awards" we gave out at our quarterly leadership summits.

It was awesome to see all of our leaders applaud their peers.

These awards meant something to people. They'd get special

placement on fireplace mantles and people would talk about them for months. It really was cool.

Appreciation like this is really powerful, because what gets rewarded gets repeated. And while this wasn't a reward for serving, it was recognition. Now I know there are questions about fairness. You might think recognizing someone who serves might not be fair to the dozens of other people who perform similar tasks.

But I believe this moment solidified the importance of volunteers and servant leaders in our church. People saw that we valued their contributions. In a way, this moment honored everyone that served. We didn't hear about jealousy or fairness, but even if we did, I would have kept doing this.

Andy Stanley says, "Do for one what you wish you could do for everyone." I've tried to adopt that in my own leadership and you should too. You may not be able to counsel everyone, but you should counsel someone. You may not be able to meet every need, but you should meet some need. You may not be able to make an appearance at every ministry event, but you should show up to support your staff at some of them. Do for one what you wish you could do for everyone and don't worry about being fair.

WE SPENT THE REST OF THE TIME DOING ONE OF FOUR THINGS

We did the leadership summit four times a year, and for the final part of our evening, each one was a little different.

At one of them, I'd present the strategic plan for the next year. Just like recognition is a powerful motivator, information can do the same thing. These were our leaders and givers. I wanted them to know where the church was headed before everyone else. And while I might do this a little bit at each of the summits, I took an extended time during one of them to talk about our big picture plans for the next year. This turned out to be a great time to cast vision.

At the next summit, we would hear from a guest speaker. I invited a few different leaders to come in and inspire or entertain our volunteers. This was always a fun time.

At the third summit of the year, we broke into groups for training. If you have volunteer teams in your church, they need basic training. But if you're like most churches, you struggle with these training meetings. They're usually not well attended. But by attaching them to our leadership summit, we were able to raise the bar and the excitement level.

The final summit of the year was a big appreciation event. We'd do the awards, but the rest of the evening was just for fun. One year, we brought in a square dance caller and had a hoe down. Another year, we did an 80's prom party. I know of several churches that do red carpet style events. These events took a little planning, but they were so much fun.

MAKE IT FIT

Would an environment like this help you inspire, appreciate, and train all of your volunteers? If so, put it on your annual calendar and start building the tradition. Take these ideas and make them your own.

You could use your quarterly leadership events to ordain deacons or elders, welcome new members, approve the budget, or participate in communion. Think through all the possibilities and consolidate your focus.

ACTION STEP

Share this chapter with your staff or some other key leaders in the church. Then talk about whether an idea like this would work for you.

- 19 -

ANNOUNCE AND CELEBRATE

Walk about Zion, go around her, number her towers, consider well her ramparts, go through her citadels, that you may tell the next generation that this is God..."

- Psalm 48:12-14 ESV -

My birthday is on September 18. Our youngest child, Matthew, was born on the same day 33 years later. Yep, we share the same birthday.

Our kids get to pick any restaurant for dinner on their birthday. Our oldest daughter always picks Red Lobster, despite the fact that I've taught her there are much better and much more real seafood restaurants out there. Our middle child usually picks Sonic because she can order a corn dog and a milkshake. Matthew sometimes picks a steakhouse. I may or may not slightly influence his decision.

With three kids, we've also organized our share of birthday parties. We've done pottery-painting parties, bowling parties, princess parties, sleepover parties, superhero parties, Star Wars parties, and more.

If it's a good party, there's a reverse present at the end. The goodie bag. This is a good idea in theory, until you realize you're spending a lot of money at the dollar store giving kids things they aren't going to use.

But there's cake. No good birthday party is complete without cake. When I was a kid, parents ordered a birthday cake from their local grocery store. The only real decision involved was the color of the icing. Today, there are a plethora of cake design ideas.

You can get a Death Star cake for your Star Wars party. You can get a Corvette cake for your Barbie party. You can get a cake in the shape of a baseball field complete with fondant baseball players for your Mets-themed party.

They didn't have cake and ice cream in the Bible days, but if they did, I'm sure they would have broken it out right after the fish and loaves.

When you read the Bible, particularly the book of Acts, you read about incredible times of celebration. For example, Acts 13 records the commissioning of Paul and Barnabus in Antioch, who were being sent out on a missionary journey to tell people about Jesus.

Acts 13:3 says, "So after they had fasted and prayed, they placed their hands on them and sent them off." This was a serious moment. These missionaries were being sent on an important mission.

In the next few chapters, you will read about their travels and their successes. They perform miracles and witness miracles. They preach amazing messages and people respond to the gospel.

Paul and Barnabus visit the city of Iconium and preach Jesus in the Jewish synagogue. Acts 14:1 says their sermons were effective and "a great number" of Jews and Greeks believed.

The story continues: "They preached the gospel in that city and won a large number of disciples. Then they returned to Lystra, Iconium and Antioch, strengthening the disciples and encouraging them to remain true to the faith."

Finally, Acts 14:27 describes their return to Antioch. "On arriving there, they gathered the church together and reported all that God had done through them and how he had opened a door of faith to the Gentiles."

I love this story from the book of Acts because it describes a complete picture. The church prayerfully sends out these missionaries. They preach the Gospel. And the church welcomes them home with a celebration.

When I read this I thought, "I need to get better at celebrating."

You see, as a visionary leader, I love looking forward. I love announcing change and leading up to it. I love every moment of the crazy activity and I love creating plans. And once the deed is done, I'm on to the next thing.

If you're a visionary leader, there's a good chance you're also driven by a compelling vision of the future. That might cause you to rush through meaningful moments in pursuit of the next great thing.

But the early church stopped to celebrate Paul and Barnabus. They spent time telling stories of God's faithfulness and goodness. It's not in the text, but I imagine them having some first century cake and ice cream.

One of my regrets as a pastor is not celebrating enough. I was so busy driving to the next event and trying to break the next barrier that I rushed through a lot of awesome moments. If I could go back and do it again, I would have celebrated more.

» I would have celebrated more when people decided to follow Jesus.

» I would have celebrated more when people were baptized.

» I would have celebrated more when people stepped into a Gospel-driven community for the first time.

» I would have celebrated when God called people away to be a part of another church or ministry.

» I would have celebrated more faithful service and volunteerism.

» I would have celebrated ordinary acts of generosity and faithful giving.

And the list goes on.

How well do you celebrate in your church? How well do your ministries celebrate wins and successes and victories? How well do you celebrate ordinary faith?

North Point Community Church does this really well with their baptism videos. When people decide to put their faith in Jesus and decide to get baptized, the church helps them tell a short version of their story on video. In fact, recording a baptism video is a requirement to be baptized at North Point.

It's a big commitment and a big investment, but I've seen firsthand how powerful it is. When the lights go down and the baptism video starts, the congregation really pays attention. Some of the stories are dramatic, but most of the stories are what most people would consider ordinary.

At the end of the video, most people thank the person who invited them to church or a small group leader or some other person who was instrumental in them meeting Jesus. This is a powerful moment. The video concludes and the person is in the baptismal waters. After they are baptized, everyone applauds. It's a time of celebration and one of my favorite parts of the church service.

You don't have to require baptism videos, but you should find a way to celebrate key decisions in your church.

Maybe you're wondering how this chapter fits in a book on organization and strategies. I'm including this because celebrating won't happen by accident.

Just like we have to plan our kid's birthday parties, we have to plan moments of celebration in our church. Everything from saying thanks to communicating wins to throwing parties should be planned and put on your master calendar.

If you spend three weeks announcing something, what if you spend three weeks on the back side telling stories and saying thanks? If you encourage volunteers to sign up and serve for a couple of weeks, what would it look like to tell stories of people who decided to serve for a few weeks after your big commitment day? What would happen if you spend just as much time thanking people who already give as you did wishing new people would start tithing?

None of this will happen by accident, particularly if it doesn't come naturally to you. So think through it all in advance and put it on your communication calendar. Devote as many emails to celebrating as you do to asking. Give just as much stage time to telling faith stories as you do to asking people to begin a faith journey.

ACTION STEP

Answer this question: What do we need to celebrate more?

- 20 -

SCHEDULE HELPFUL EMAILS

You don't lead by hitting people over the head—that's assault, not leadership.

– Dwight Eisenhower –

I subscribe to several church email lists because I love knowing what God is doing in churches around the world. And in my line of work, it's a good way to stay current with church trends.

This means I read a ton of church announcements. There are pretty graphics describing a new series. I hear all the details for those special events. A lot of information hits my inbox. But rarely do I receive something that helps me grow in my faith. I hear a lot of announcements, but I rarely hear anything that can truly help my family.

Most churches are missing a golden opportunity.

It's time we stop sending emails to make announcements and instead use them as a tool to pastor people. I'm not talking about fancy newsletters or information blasts. Those rarely connect with people.

I'm talking about using emails as a tool to pastor people. Even though social media has exploded in popularity, email is still one of the most reliable, cost effective ways to send helpful information to the people you lead.

Take a look at your last several email blasts. Are they about your church or the person receiving them? Are they full of announcements about your church or do they help people in their life?

When you broaden your gaze, you'll see dozens of ways you can use email in a much more effective way. You can use emails to actually pastor people. For example:

» You can use emails to authentically connect with your congregation to let them in on parts of your life. Instead of cold newsletters from the church perspective, write in the first person and let people in on your life.

» You can use emails to share helpful resources to help people grow on their own. Why not send helpful articles, links, and resources or the kind of stuff you'd include in a sermon?

» Why not use email to encourage people to give, serve, or get in a group? I'm not talking about announcements. I'm talking about personal reasons.

Personal, authentic email communication is a powerful tool you can use to pastor your congregation. It can be an extension of your pastoral ministry, not just a digital version of your bulletin.

Instead of blasting information, you can send authentic notes and helpful content. Use all the tools at your disposal, including email, to make disciples.

To get you thinking, here's a sample email you might send to your church. It's not full of announcements, but it's a personal invitation to read the Bible.

SAMPLE EMAIL

James,

My powers of persuasion rarely work on my kids. But I'm hoping for better results today. I'll be straight with you—I want to talk you into doing something.

I'm hoping to convince you to read the Bible every day this week for seven days in a row. Here are three reasons I think you should:

1. *There's interesting stuff in the Bible. Don't ever let someone tell you the Bible is boring. If someone says that, they aren't reading it right. Noah's Ark, David and Goliath, Samson and Delilah, wars and conquest, love and marriage, Peter cutting off a soldier's ear, a dead man coming back to life...I could go on and on. There are some incredible stories in the Bible.*

2. *The Bible is unlike any other book. This might surprise you, but the Bible isn't really a book at all. It's a collection of 66 small books or letters. It was written by*

40 different authors across a couple of continents and in three languages. It has been collected, organized, and preserved for us.

3. *The Bible has influenced the world like no other book. The Bible has shaped more than just preachers. It has influenced Presidents and Kings.*

I know it's overwhelming, but did you know that if you read for just 15 minutes a day, you can read the whole Bible in about a year? If you read God's Word for just 15 minutes a day, I think you will benefit.

SO, WHERE DO I START?

I know this sounds weird, but if you want to start reading the Bible, I don't recommend starting at the beginning. (I told you the Bible wasn't like other books...can you imagine starting a novel from the middle?)

If I were you, I'd start with the New Testament, specifically the Gospel of John. It's all about the life of Jesus, and it was written by one of his best friends.

So what do you say? Will you give it a try?

Pastor Chris

P.S. If you want to read online, here's a great website. You can follow a reading plan or just dive into the Book of John.

You can use email to share what God is doing in your life. You can use email to share resources and ideas to parents. You can use email to point people to resources that can help them grow in their faith. Let your church know about community functions, sports leagues, and events that need volunteers. This kind of information is really helpful.

It's a powerful tool. Use it well.

ACTION STEP

Pull together a group of people and brainstorm a list of helpful things that you could email your entire congregation. If you want a jumpstart, you can download 12 helpful emails from churchfuel.com/streamline

- 21 -

COMMUNICATE WITH YOUR DONORS

Donor loyalty is not about the donor being loyal to you, it is you being loyal to the donor.

– Harvey McKinnon –

There are few topics that scare pastors, such as raising money. After all, you were neither called nor trained to be a professional fundraiser.

But money is a spiritual issue.

Jesus said people's money and hearts were connected. That makes money a spiritual issue, not just a financial one. That makes stewardship a part of the discipleship process.

You cannot make disciples without getting into financial stewardship. And you cannot lead a healthy and growing church without leading people into generosity. These two things go hand in hand. In more ways than one, the stakes are high.

One of the most critical things you can do in your first year is create a healthy culture of stewardship and generosity. This involves financial accountability and good systems. But it also requires an intentional approach to talking about money.

Don't abdicate spiritual leadership by refusing to talk about money in a healthy way.

In addition to being a spiritual entrepreneur, pastor and counselor, and outreach specialist, you are also a fundraiser. Many planters shy away from this reality, deciding to delegate financial responsibility to a group of people. Maybe it's a lack of training or maybe it's abuse, but too many church planters don't see raising the financial temperature of the young church as their responsibility. However, this cannot be delegated. You must lead well in this area, and in order to do so, you must talk about money.

OBJECTIONS TO TALKING ABOUT MONEY

1. It takes time for new Christians to understand giving.

I've heard this from many planters, and while it's a reality, it can easily become an excuse. If you're reaching unchurched people, it will take time to create a culture of stewardship with new converts. But this culture will take a lot longer if you don't have an intentional plan to teach it. You cannot rush discipleship, but refusing to address the topics out of the fear that people will leave is neither helpful nor wise.

2. Unchurched people don't want to hear about money issues.

The idea of talking about money in a brand new church might sound counterproductive to the mission. After all, the unchurched people you are trying to reach don't want to hear about money.

So we avoid the topic. It's true that unchurched people don't want to be forced by guilt into giving to an organization they don't yet know or trust. But unchurched people aren't dumb. They know it takes money to run a church.

If you limit your fundraising efforts to people who attend church consistently, you're missing out on as much as 75% of the population. Generosity is attractive. Imagine how people living in the first century thought of those early Christians. They were known for their generosity, not just their theology.

Unchurched people don't hate the idea of generosity. They give all the time, just not to the local church. Your mission is to communicate the vision, and explain the why behind the what.

3. I'm not a money guy.

As we discussed earlier, stewardship is a discipleship issue. You might not have a degree in accounting or business management, but as a shepherd of a local church, you have a responsibility to help people follow Jesus. And as a leader responsible for the overall health of the organization, you owe it to the mission to lead well. Don't let your personality become an organizational deficiency.

THREE TIMES YOU NEED TO TALK ABOUT MONEY

Let's say you're convinced money is a spiritual issue and you need to create a healthy plan to talk about money. You believe this will help people follow Jesus and help your young church build a sustainable ministry in the community. So now what? Exactly what do you do?

A healthy, effective, and balanced approach to talking about money in a church takes planning. By looking at a calendar and building a solid communication plan, you can build a healthy culture instead of responding to an impending crisis. Here are three times you should intentionally talk about money in church:

1. Talk about money every week.

Weekly Whoa...you just lost me. There's no way I'm preaching on money every week!

If you receive an offering every week, you're already mentioning money every week. I just want you to make this time more meaningful. Every week when you receive an offering, you have the opportunity to cast a vision for your church. Besides, passing the plates after a rushed prayer or a shallow speech isn't clear to guests.

Before you receive an offering, take one or two minutes and explain the "why behind the what." Use Scripture, testimonies, video, and creativity to connect the dots for people. Here are some ideas about what you might say:

> » In just a few minutes, we're going to receive an offering. It's something we do every week here at Cross Church, and here's why...

> » Every week, we receive an offering and it helps make all of this possible. Today, I just wanted to let you know what we do with the money you give. Forty-two cents of every dollar goes to...

> » Do you know there are actually four other services happening right now? All over this building, children are learning about Jesus. Your gifts make this possible...

> » Before our ushers pass the plate and we receive an offering,

I just wanted to share this verse with you...

> » In just a minute, ushers are going to pass the plate and people from all walks of life are going to make donations to the church. Before we do that, I wanted to show you this video of the impact this church is having on one family...

I bet if you spent one hour on this, you could think of 15-20 creative, inspiring, and effective ways to set up the offering time in your church. You might even be able to blend in an important announcement. Once you've got them down on paper, put them in your communication calendar.

You're already receiving an offering, so why not make it more meaningful to those who give, and more effective at the same time? You're going to use words to explain it, so why not connect those words to something of importance?

You can take the preaching calendar and the communication calendar and add this information to it. Plan these moments just like you plan all the other moments in your service.

2. Cast vision to your donors every quarter.

Most churches send annual contribution statements to everyone who made a contribution during a calendar year. Most of the time, these are lifeless statements sent because the Federal Government requires them. You can take something ordinary and make it special. You can make this annual contribution statement something inspiring and meaningful.

But let's take this to the next level. Why not send an update on a quarterly basis? The government asks you do this once a year, but why let the government determine the minimum standard for vision casting in your church?

Non-profits around the world know the power of communicating with their donor base, but local churches leave so many opportunities on the table. The people who contribute to your church need to hear from you more than once a year. Whether it's through snail mail or email, craft a unique and inspirational communication piece and let donors know what they have given and what's happening with their donations. Here are some ideas:

» Send a video recap of ministry highlights along with a PDF of a donor's giving statement.

» Let children in your children's ministry write thank you notes to those who help make ministry happen.

» Turn a baptism picture into a refrigerator magnet and send it to all of your donors with a thank you note.

» Send a letter encouraging donors to set up automated, recurring contributions.

» Pull your staff or key volunteers together and write personalized thank you notes to accompany a giving statement.

Four times a year, communicate with your donors. Say thanks. Give information. Cast vision.

3. Preach a stewardship series every year.

Jesus had a lot to say on the subject of money, so it should frequently show up in your preaching. But once a year, spend an extended period of time talking about money. Spend three to five weeks on the topic, and cover it from all angles. Remember, it's not just a giving issue, it's a heart issue.

Your stewardship series should not just be about giving money to the church. You can also help people with their finances. You can talk about spending, savings, and debt. You can preach on the broader issue of stewardship. You can offer people help and hope.

But during this series, you should intentionally ask people to give to the church. Don't shy away from it and don't apologize for talking about something Jesus said was important. Be clear and be bold.

Every week, every quarter and every year you have the opportunity to talk about money. You can put this on a calendar and treat it like a system. The plan will give you a framework to create a healthy culture, and it will keep your communication on track.

There's so much involved in building a healthy stewardship ministry at church, but it all starts with clear communication. Learn how to communicate with donors and potential churches and you will create traction in the area of generosity.

ACTION STEP

One of the best ways to build long-term traction is to create a healthy financial situation in your church. We've put together a course that will help you create a gameplan for raising and managing money. It's called The Systems Course and you can find it at churchfuel.com. It's one of the best investments you can make in leading a healthy church.

- 22 -

FOLLOW UP WITH FIRST TIME GUESTS

People will forget what you said.
They will forget what you did.
But they will never forget how you made them feel.

– Maya Angelou –

I've got good news and I've got bad news.

You *will* have first time guests visit your church.

Even churches that don't *try* to reach new people acquire a few first time guests. But just because people show up on Sunday doesn't mean they're going to stick. Whether or not they get involved depends on a variety of factors.

It takes a combination of people and processes to create a culture that's guest friendly and connects guests into the life of the church. Just think of all the steps that must happen in order for a new person to get connected:

» They hear about your church.

» They hear about your church again.

» Someone invites them to a service.

» They visit your website looking for more information or service times.

» They find what they're looking for on your website.

» They decide to visit on a Sunday.

» They actually visit on a Sunday.

» They park a car and walk toward the door, with lots of uneasy feelings running through their head.

» They check in their kids, with a lot more uneasy feelings running through their head.

» They fill out a connection card during the service or at some type of information center.

» They pick up their kids and make their way to the car.

» They formally or informally evaluate their experience, rating absolutely everything from the friendliness of the people to the music and the message.

» They ask their kids if they had a good time and their kids respond to the question.

» They get some type of post-attendance communication, either an email or a form letter or a note.

» They decide to come back.

» They meet someone or a group of people.

In this chapter, I want to give you some practical ideas for how to connect guests to the life of the church and help them to follow Jesus.

PART ONE:
GETTING GUEST FRIENDLY

Before we talk about following up with guests, we need to back up a step and talk about getting guest friendly.

A lot of churches come to me because they need help with systems and strategies. When I ask about their needs, many tell me they have a problem assimilating people or closing the back door.

First, I'd like to propose that we all stop using the word assimilation when talking about people and the church. I can't imagine anyone wants to be assimilated into anything. It sounds like Star Trek, as if your goal is to strip away any unique identity and make someone look and act like everyone on the inside. Of course, that's not your goal, so let's use a simpler term.

If you want to *connect* people to the life of your church, you're going to need an intentional process to relationally turn a first time guest into a regular attender. You'll need another one to turn a regular attender into an involved member.

But here's the thing: Connection problems usually start before someone visits your church. You've got to do some hard work to get guest friendly.

So before we talk about advertising or outreach or getting more people through the front doors, let's talk about what they're going to experience when they visit.

Here's the question I want to ask.

IS IT CLEAR?

Is everything that happens at your church *clear* to potential guests? Does everything make sense to people who have no inside information about your church? Guests have no prior knowledge about how your church works, and this is something that's easy to forget.

Think about the language you use in your sermons and announcements. It all might make sense to you, but there's a good chance it's not entirely guest friendly. For example:

» Do you have a sign that points to "Higher Ground" or "The Sunshine Class?" While church members might know what those things mean, a first time guest has no idea.

» Do you use the word "tithe" in your service? If you do, you assume people know what that means. I'm not suggesting you throw out the word, but if you use it you should explain it.

» Does your sermon assume prior Bible knowledge? If you say something like, "You know...like it says in 2 John..." even in passing, you've unintentionally communicated there are two kinds of people at church—those who know what 2 John is and those who don't.

» If you talk about "KidZone" do guests know what you mean?

» Do your screen announcements, bulletin, welcome, communication card, and signs all make sense to someone with no prior knowledge of your church?

I'm not talking about watering down the message or changing your theology. I'm simply recommending that you explain anything out of the ordinary to people who have no insider knowledge about your church.

You might think you're being clear. But if you want a real answer to this question, you've got to ask an outsider. You've got to bring in a secret shopper. You've got to get feedback from an actual first-timer. At minimum, visit your website, walk around your facility, and watch your service intentionally looking for things that aren't clear to outsiders.

ARE YOU TALKING TO GUESTS?

Even if you know everyone in the room by name and are certain they have been members of your church for at least a decade, you should still go out of your way to address first time guests in your service.

Why? Because you're creating a mindset.

You're reinforcing the idea that first-time guests should be present. This is no small thing because a guest mindset leads to a guest friendly church.

One of the best places to speak directly to guests is during the welcome. Toward the beginning of every church service, someone should take the stage and simply welcome everyone. You're a tour guide and this is your opportunity to make guests feel welcome. Here's an example of something you might say:

> Hello everyone. My name is Chris and I'm the Small Groups Pastor here at BridgeWater Church. Thanks so much for being here.
>
> If today is your first time, we're REALLY glad you're here. I know there are ton of places you could be today, and we're honored you would choose to spend it with us. You may not have realized this before now, but a lot of what we're going to do today is designed just for you....our special guest.
>
> One of the most important things you need to know about is our mission. We're here to lead people from where they are to where God wants them to be. So no matter where you are, we're glad you're here.
>
> Now, here's what's going to happen this morning. In just a minute, we're going to sing a few songs. The words will be up on the screen and it's totally okay if you're not a singer. After that, our senior Pastor, Chris, is going to continue a teaching series from the book of Ephesians. We'll put all the key points and Bible verses up here on the screen.
>
> Finally, at the end of the service, we'll do something we do every week...receive an offering. If you want to financially support the church, that's the time to do it. We'll talk more about that later.
>
> Now one last thing. If you are a guest with us today, we have a gift for you. It's one of these coffee mugs right here. Just stop by

*the Welcome Center on your way out and one of our volunteers
will be happy to give you one.*

*Whether you're brand new or whether you've been here for a
while let us know if you have any questions. We're here to serve
you all. Now, why don't we all stand up and say hi to someone
near you. Then our band will lead a few songs.*

I recommend you say something like that *every* week. Yes, your
regular attenders won't pay attention after a few weeks, but this
part of the service isn't for them. It's for those who are attending
for the first time. Treat them with respect and let them know what's
happening. It's what you'd do if you had guests visit your home.

All of this is a part of getting guest friendly—handling everything
in a way that makes sense to guests.

PART TWO:
DESIGNING A FOLLOW UP SYSTEM

A lot of churches are investing serious money in advertising and
outreach events these days. You can do Facebook marketing, direct
mail, and special events to reach people in your community and let
them know about your church.

But before you spend one dollar on advertising, there's a second
thing you need to do. In addition to getting guest friendly on the
front end, you need to design a follow up system that will work on
the back end.

Think about it. You get to pre-determine, to a large degree, what guests experience when they actually visit your church.

The time to work on this is *before* people show up. If you decide what you want guests to experience in advance and create a system to ensure it happens, there's a greater likelihood that first time guests will have a good experience.

The principle we're going to build on in this chapter applies to a variety of actions people take in church.

Actions should trigger steps.

> » Every time someone gives money to your church for the very first time, a first time donor follow up process should kick in.

> » Every time someone begins a relationship with Jesus Christ, your process for following up with new believers should automatically guide them to their next step.

> » Every time someone visits your church for the first time, it should trigger a first time guest follow up process.

So have you intentionally designed a follow up experience? Let me walk you through some key steps.

KEY MOMENT #1:
GETTING INFORMATION

If you want to follow up with first-time guests, you need a good way to collect their information. Given the fact that privacy issues are a concern for so many, this is no small task. Here are some good ways to obtain the information from first time guests:

First, you might use a connection card or communication card in your service. This is pretty common, but with a few tweaks, you might be able to dramatically improve your response rate.

» Spend one or two minutes in your service talking about the communication card. Even if your regular people have heard it before, explain the card to guests. Don't assume people will fill it out...ask them to do it.

» Let people know what you're going to do with their information. When you're explaining your connection card, let people know *why* you're asking for this information and what you're going to do with it. Most guests don't want to be added to a mailing list, so communicate a benefit to people. You might say, "If you share your information with us, we'd love to ask for your feedback or send you a special gift."

» Ask for as little information as possible. I've always wondered why some churches ask for the ages of kids and what schools they attend. While this might be interesting to know, it's not important. Every request for additional information will cut down your overall response rate, so only ask for what's necessary. A lot of churches are only asking for name, email address, and phone number. Less is more.

Secondly, you might offer first time guests a special gift for visiting. During your welcome, you could invite people to drop their connection card into the offering bucket. That's pretty common. But you could also ask them to take it to a designated area in the lobby and receive a special gift.

We used this approach and it worked really well. Not only were we able to obtain more connection cards, we were also able to strike up conversations with people. This was a big win for our church.

KEY MOMENT #2:
IMMEDIATE FOLLOW UP

Once you obtain people's information, what are you going to do with it? Remember, you get to design their follow up experience in advance, so think through what you want people to receive. One of the best ways to answer this question is to ask yourself what *you* would like to receive from a church if you visited.

The form letter is the most common form of follow up, but it's also the least personal and the least effective. Think about it...how many form letters do *you* enjoy reading? Personally, I'd rather receive a three sentence, personalized email than a form letter.

Another option is to send a personalized note card. In this day of email, status updates, and tweets, personal notes sent with a stamp really stand out. Personal notes are memorable and people often save them as they know you didn't cut and paste the message. They communicate value because people know they take time to send. And they can really make someone's day.

Depending on your culture, you might find that a phone call or text message is a great way to follow up with people who visit your church.

KEY MOMENT #3:
ONGOING COMMUNICATION

I'm slowly seeing churches adopt successful strategies from businesses and other non profit organizations. One such strategy is automated email marketing.

When a first-time guest visits your church and provides their email address, that action can "trigger" a pre-determined sequence of emails from the pastor. You can set up these emails to be automatically delivered over the course of a few weeks, and while they're automatically sent, they're sent from a real person's email address.

Email sequences are a great way to spread out important information about the church and begin a conversation with a new person.

Most churches don't do this. Instead, they simply add a person to the church database and start speaking to them just like everyone else. Instead of intentional communication to a guest, they might hear about programs and events that make little sense. Instead of a welcome message from the pastor, they might get invited to the church work day.

Imagine crafting a series of five emails you can automatically send to everyone who attends your church. The first email might thank them for visiting and ask if they have any questions. The next email might introduce the pastor and his family—most guests never get this information. A third email might describe the *regular* programs and events and how they might benefit a new person.

The possibilities are endless and email provides an opportunity to create real conversations with guests.

CREATING YOUR SYSTEM

The key is to decide what you're going to do when people visit and create the system to make sure it happens. Make the decision in advance and then execute your plan.

Like all systems, you should capture your system in a document or illustration. Write it down so you can visualize it. It's hard to evaluate a system that only exists in your head, so capture everything in a simple flow chart.

ACTION STEP

Use flowchart software like Omnigraffle or a whiteboard to draw out your guest follow up process. Decide what's going to happen, when it is going to happen, and who is going to make sure it happens.

[First Time Guest] Follow Up System

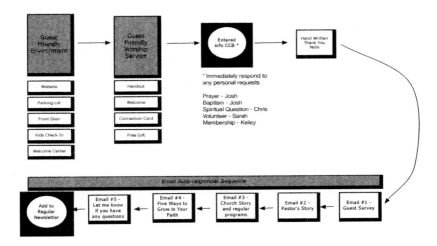

Figure 7. Guest Follow Up Processes illustrated in a flow chart. You can download this file for free at churchfuel.com/streamline.

- 23 -

COMMUNICATE MISSION AND VISION

By far the most effective way to turn fear into confidence is to be clear; to define the future in such vivid terms, through your actions, words, images, pictures, heroes, and scores that we can all see where you, and thus we, are headed.

– Marcus Buckingham –

There's no greater discussed topic in church leadership than vision. Blogs, books, and podcasts are filled with all kinds of content. For as long as I can remember, this has been a buzzword for pastors. Everybody wants to talk about vision.

When I was a church planter, I read extensively on mission, vision, purpose, values, and strategy. I went through workshops that led me through all kinds of processes to help clarify our vision and communicate our purpose. Honestly, it became a little overwhelming.

There was a big part of me that wanted to put down the dry erase marker and just do something. I didn't get into ministry to argue the semantics between a purpose statement, a mission statement, and a vision statement.

It wasn't until much later in ministry when I realized the power of a compelling mission and a clear vision, and the difference between those two things. In fact, this realization was a light bulb moment for me.

WHAT IS A MISSION STATEMENT?

There are a lot of articles and books to help you craft a mission statement, and the last thing I want to do is regurgitate best practices. But there's something important here and I don't want you to miss it.

Peter Drucker says the first question every leader should ask is: "What is our mission?" Simon Sinek says you must start with why, not what. What these great writers are talking about is mission.

A mission statement describes the overall reason your church exists. Some people call this a purpose statement, but the bottom line is you must be able to articulate in one sentence the reason your church is here.

This isn't a job for a random committee and it's not a box to check so you can get funding. It's a crucial part of your ministry. You must be able to articulate the reason you do what you do. As you're working on this, keep these two things in mind.

Firstly, your mission statement is going to come from the pages of Scripture. Despite all the focus on being unique, it's really the

Great Commission that should guide your church. You can say it in a creative way, but creating disciples should be at the heart of your church. Helping people love God and love others is really what the church should be about.

Secondly, your mission statement is going to come from your heart. Whether you have a formal statement or not, your mission lives in your heart. It's going to be your mission before you craft a statement, or else it won't be real. In a way, mission statements are discovered not created.

This is why you shouldn't import your mission statement from another church. There are enough churches with mission statements imported from Northpoint with core values stolen from Elevation Church. It's great to be inspired by other great churches, but mission (and vision, as we're going to see) need to come from Scripture through your unique personality and circumstances.

As you wrestle through your calling, your community, and your culture, you and your team should work hard to crystalize your mission into a memorable statement. Great statements are both concise and precise.

People aren't going to remember a two-paragraph mission statement. And if they can't remember or recite it, it stands little chance of impacting them. Use as few words as possible to communicate as much as possible. Your mission statement isn't the place to describe your core values, key beliefs or main activities. It should be short enough to fit on a t-shirt or be shared from memory via social media.

To get you thinking, here are some examples of good church mission statements. I don't share these so you can copy them, but to give you an example of how you can create a short, memorable statement to help people understand why you exist:

» Christ Church of the Valley: To *win* people to Jesus Christ, *train* believers to become disciples, and *send* disciples out to impact the world.

» Willow Creek Community Church in Chicago, Illinois: Turning irreligious people into fully devoted followers of Christ.

» Missio Dei Church in Cincinnati, Ohio: To see the people of Cincinnati forever changed by the Gospel of Jesus and holding dear to Him as their source of all joy and worth.

» Christ Church of the King in Brighton, England: To be a Christ-centered Church in an influential City, which multiplies and helps other Churches towards these shared goals, across the region, Western Europe, and beyond.

Creating a great statement is one thing, but communicating it is another. Once you have a clear and compelling mission statement, talk about it everywhere. Here are some ideas.

» Use it during the welcome time in your service

» Put it on the home page of your website

» Include it in your email signature

» Print it on the front page of your bulletin

» Paint it on the walls of your lobby

» Overlay it on top of pictures of people being baptized

» Write it in thank you notes you send to donors

» Preach an entire message series on it

» Turn it into a video and show it at the very beginning of your service.

WHAT IS A VISION STATEMENT?

Your mission statement is an important foundational piece of your church. It's a statement that summarizes your "why." It encapsulates your reason for existence.

But there's another statement you need.

A few years ago, my wife and I decided we wanted to give our kids a broader experience of the world. We love to travel and experience new cultures, and we wanted our children to learn more about the world.

Since I could work from anywhere, we decided to rent a house in a different city and experience life there. We'd connect with a church and get to know the people. Wouldn't it be memorable for our kids if they had several summers like this? What would it do for their worldview if they were exposed to different cultures?

So we made a list of cities we could live in for a month or six weeks during the summer—New York, Hong Kong, London, Jerusalem, and Nairobi. It would be more than a vacation but less disruptive than moving there.

We talked to our kids and they liked the idea. We talked about what we hoped they would experience and learn. We talked about the why. All of this goes in the "purpose" category. At this point, the plan was purposeful, but it was still general.

Then we started our research. It turns out there are several Home Exchange websites where you can swap houses with people all over the world. There are companies that help with short-term rentals. And there are lots of churches who would welcome a family for a month.

In the end, we settled on Baltimore for our first experience. It was within driving distance, so travel was cheaper. And I knew a great church there doing inner city work. We rented a row house close to the harbor and lived there for a month.

Purpose turned into vision. Instead of talking about the why, we were able to talk with our kids about where we were going and what we were going to do. We moved from purpose to vision. The conversation switched from generic to specific. Purpose meant giving our kids new life experiences. Vision meant moving to Baltimore for the month of July and helping Captivate Church.

On May 25, 1961, President John F. Kennedy delivered a special address to congress on the importance of space travel. In this speech, he didn't just talk about America's mission to visit space. He cast a specific vision—to put a man on the moon and safely return him by the end of the decade.

He gave a timeline. He discussed dollars. It wasn't just a mission; it was a vision.

Your church needs a mission statement, but you also need a statement that describes your vision.

THE DIFFERENCE BETWEEN MISSION AND VISION

Hopefully, you're beginning to understand there's a huge difference between mission and vision. But let's dive a little deeper into the differences.

» Your mission is never really accomplished. Making disciples or loving your community or sending missionaries is a life-long job, and you're probably never going to see it totally accomplished in your lifetime. So in this way, your mission is never really accomplished. It's a constant goal and it's always there. But your vision should be accomplished in a specific amount of time. It's something you should be able to check off. Teaching my kids is a life-long pursuit, but arriving in Baltimore should happen by a certain time and date. Exploring space is never-ending, but putting a man on the moon by the end of the decade can be checked off a list.

» Your mission is really about the direction your church is headed. Reaching the world, sharing the Gospel, and serving the community describe the direction your church is heading. But your vision is about what the destination looks like. Casting a vision paints a very real picture of the future.

» When it comes to mission, nearly all Christians should agree. There will always be one or two who disagree with anything, but for the most part, all Christians can agree on the mission of making disciples. We might debate strategy, however the mission is pretty clear. But not everyone should agree or buy into your specific vision. Your vision gets into strategy, and this should actually create a dividing line for some people. This doesn't create a lack of unity; it creates focus.

» Your mission might sound something like, "We're here to glorify God and make disciples." But your vision will be far more specific. It might sound like, "We're going to launch three campuses in the next three years."

If you want to rally people to action, you must communicate mission and vision. Talking about your mission will keep people inspired, but talking about your vision will keep people focused.

I'm convinced most churches have a mission but very few have a clear vision. Do a simple Google search and you'll see that most vision statements are really mission statements. They are generic, not specific.

Successful churches talk about the mission and vision until everyone is on the same page and headed in that direction.

ACTION STEP

Write down your mission and vision. If you can't do it from memory or it's not clear and compelling, ask someone for help and get to work.

- 24 -

A WARNING ABOUT SYSTEMS, PROCESSES, AND STRUCTURE

Never quit something with great long-term potential just because you can't deal with the stress of the moment.

– Seth Godin –

I'm a huge believer in creating healthy systems in any organization. After all, I just wrote a book on it. Most problems are really systems problems, and if we address the systems, we solve the resulting problems.

However, *relying* on systems is also problematic. In fact, an organization that has smooth systems could be in just as much danger as the disorganized organization. (Is that an oxymoron?)

So in conclusion, I want to challenge you to implement but not rely on everything I wrote in this book. It's entirely possible, maybe even likely, to become *too* systematized. Here's what I mean.

1. SYSTEMS CAN CREATE A FALSE PLUG AND PLAY MENTALITY

You see one church do something well and you adopt their system. The problem here is failing to recognize your unique mission and personalities. You don't lead the same way as that other guy, and you've got different people.

I can show you dozens of organizations that fell by the wayside trying to copy their larger competition and implement their systems.

How many churches have tried to copy Willow Creek, and in the end realized that they didn't have Bill Hybels at the helm? How many churches have tried to copy Passion City, only to realize that they didn't have the same level of talent on their team?

You can't import vision or passion, and a system created for one culture might not work in yours.

But that's the good news. God wants to do something unique through you and your church and your community. The world doesn't need you to be a clone or for your church to be a carbon copy.

2. SYSTEMS CAN CREATE AN UNHEALTHY RELIANCE ON MAN-MADE METHODS, RATHER THAN A RELIANCE ON GOD

The bottom line is that systems work! And as they work and as you see results, you might be tempted to rely on methods rather than depend on God. Focusing on methods can cause you to miss the bigger picture—the reason you went into ministry in the first place.

By all means, create healthy systems, and bring in outsiders who can speak into the process. But don't *rely* on those systems. Prepare your horse for the day of battle, but recognize the victory comes from God.

3. SYSTEMS CAN BECOME AN EXCUSE FOR A LACK OF RELATIONAL LEADERSHIP

A computer screen is my comfort zone.

And I like my desk. I'd be perfectly happy behind a closed door surrounded by books and connected to blogs.

Such is the life of an introvert.

But my personality quickly turned into an obstacle, and I failed to realize this important lesson:

Leadership involves people, not just paper.

While strategies are helpful (in fact, I believe they're essential) I allowed myself to get lost in them and missed the bigger picture.

Musicians are not going to be developed via twitter. You can put out a twitter APB for bass players, and someone may respond. But frequent calls for help is a sign that there isn't a culture built on relationship and mission.

You cannot make disciples via Facebook. You can find out which Kardashian you are most like, or join the pirate army in the fight against the Sith Lords, or maybe even discuss that obscure Old Testament passage in the One Hundred Million Christians Strong Studying the Old Testament Group, but for all the connection opportunities Facebook offers people , real life doesn't happen online. It might be a window into life, but it's not real life.

If you're going to make a difference, it's going to take conversations. You're going to have to push back from your desk, leave the confines of your keyboard, and go out there and talk to people.

Systems can lull you into acting like the Wizard of Oz, directing from behind the curtain but never getting to know anyone. However, it's impossible to lead via email or through a document. The danger of systems is thinking that they replace relationships.

4. SYSTEMS CAN KEEP YOU FROM LEADING AND KNOWING REAL PEOPLE WITH REAL PROBLEMS

Once more, I'm speaking from personal experience. The people under my leadership were not impressed with my 12-week planning process or event planning checklist.

Those systems, no matter how clear and effective, didn't help anyone. New healthy systems should create a culture that makes helping people simpler, but they cannot replace getting your hands dirty.

Every need doesn't fit nicely into a category. People aren't going to be helped with your flowcharts and manuals.

This is not a push back on organization or a criticism of installing systems. We need those things. Most of us need *more* of those things. But systems are a means to the end, not the end itself.

CONCLUSION

In 1991, I walked down the aisle at First Baptist Church in Jacksonville, Florida to surrender to full time Christian ministry. I didn't totally understand those terms, or the ramifications of that decision. But I remember a strong pull to abandon my desire to be a lawyer and work in a local church.

The next thing I remember was the pastor mispronouncing my name as he shared my decision with about 3,000 people. (It's *Loo-kah-zoo-sk*i, by the way.)

Ever since then, I've never been able to escape the pull of the local church. Looking back on my life, it's *full* of local church influence. Here are just a few reasons I give my time, energy, and passion to helping local churches:

1. A local church helped set the trajectory of my life. When I was 15, I decided to follow Jesus with my life at a local church. My best friends were members of that same church, and we all stood in each other's weddings. I met my wife because of that church.

2. Most pastors are selfless servants who want to make a difference. In my line of work, I've had the opportunity to interact with hundreds, probably even thousands of pastors. And most of them are amazing, humble, selfless leaders who love Jesus and love their communities. Pastors are heroes.

3. Churches come in all shapes and sizes. There are rural churches and urban churches. There are progressive churches and traditional churches. There are small churches and mega churches. All of them are important and all of them matter. I know there is still work to do, but local congregations all over the world reflect heaven and their community at the same time. That is amazing.

4. The church is the closest representation of Jesus we have on earth. Jesus is invisible, and I've never been to heaven. But the church is the body of Christ, and I can see that. When local churches love and serve their community, worship wholeheartedly, and give generously, it's a very real picture of Jesus.

5. Every church member is family. What unites us is far greater than what divides us. Everyone who is a part of a local church is a part of the universal church. That makes them family. They might be more like the crazy great Uncle, but it's family nevertheless.

6. Jesus said He would build His church. Jesus told Peter He would build His *church*. Not a 501(c)3 non profit organization. Or a publishing company. Or the Boy Scouts. He said He would build His Church. Lots of things matter, but there was a guy who was dead and came back to life. I'm going to hitch up to his construction crew and help build what He's building.

There's a lot you *could* do, but you've chosen to serve the local church. That's honorable, impressive, and amazing!

APPENDIX:
RESOURCE LIST

Download all of these documents and resources for free at churchfuel.com/streamline

» **Annual Calendar Template** – This Excel calendar template will help you look at an entire year in the life of your church.

» **Preaching Calendar Template** – Use this Excel document to plan your preaching for the next twelve months.

» **Org Chart** – This OmniGraffle file can be quickly changed and customized to document the leadership structure in your church.

» **Employee Handbook** – This is a document to cover important personnel issues in your church. It's a good idea to review it each year and make sure everyone on your team is up to speed on current policies.

» **Hiring Process** – This document will give you a framework to hire people in your church. Each step of the process is covered in detail, and there's a job profile and interview questions as well.

» **Staff Clarity Worksheet** – Part of your job at Chief Clarity Officer is to clarify roles and goals for everyone on your team. This Excel document will help you document everything. Once it's complete, share it with everyone and keep everyone on the same page.

» **Personal Leadership Development Plan** – Use this as inspiration to decide how you're going to grow as a leader. Remember, plans trump goals every time.

» **Performance Review** – This form will help you do official performance reviews. You fill out a copy and the employee fills out a copy. Then you get together and talk.

» **Meeting Rhythm Video** – This coaching video will help you and your team understand the meeting rhythm used by many successful organizations.

» **Volunteer Job Description** – Every volunteer in your church should have a simple, written job description. This template will help you get started.

» **12 Emails** - You can send pastoral emails to your church, and these 12 emails are a good start. Cut, paste, customize and send.

» **Guest Follow Up Flow Chart** – This OmniGraffle flowchart shows you how to follow up with a first time guest at your church. Of course, you should change it to match your priorities.